MW01461900

Security Operation Center – Analyst Guide

SIEM Technology Use Cases and Practices

INTRODUCTION	1
MODULE 1 - SECURITY OPERATIONS CENTER FUNDAMENTALS	7
Why do we need a SOC?	9
SOC Challenges	9
Amount of Data	9
Numerous End-points and Billions of Logs	11
Sophisticated Attacks	12
Regulatory Compliance Requirements	12
SOC Services	13
Continuous Threat Monitoring and Incident Detection	14
Incident Response	14
Threat Mitigation	14
Rule/Signature Updates	15
Threat Intelligence Integration	15
Constituency	16
SOC Roles and Teams	16
SOC Topology	19
SOC Reports	20
In-House SOC vs Outsourced SOC	21
Outsourced SOC – Service Level Agreements	23
SOC Analyst – Desired Skill Set	25
SOC Roles	27
Security Analyst	
SME/ Research Specialist	28
SOC Manager	29
Chief Information Security Officer (CISO)	29
Information Needed by SOC Roles	30
Review Questions	31

MODULE 2 - SIEM SELECTION AND DEPLOYMENT — 35

How to Select an SIEM Solution? — 37
- Ease of Deployment — 37
- Ease of Data Accessibility — 38
- Provision for Threat Intelligence Integration — 38
- Tools — 40
- Types of Reports — 40

SOC Metrics — 40
How to Select SIEM — 42
SOC Functional Modules — 45
- Event Generators — 46
- Sensors – Expected Qualities — 47
- Event Collectors — 48
- Event protocol — 49
- Collector to Source Communication Protocol — 51
- API based –MSWMI — 51
- Microsoft Security Event Log Over MSRPC Protocol — 52
- WinRM — 52
- SDEE — 54
- Challenges or Risks in Building a SOC — 55
- Humans — 55
- Processes and Procedures — 56
- Legacy and Technologies — 56
- Noise — 57
- Technical — 57
- **Review Questions** — 59

MODULE 3 - MANAGED SECURITY SERVICES SLA — 62
MSSP Service Level Agreement — 64
- Assessing an SLA — 65

Managed Security Services SLA Sample	66
Access Control Performance Matrix and Assured Deliverables	70
Boundary Defenses Performance Matrix and Assured Deliverables	73
Network and System Resource Integrity Performance Matrix and Assured Deliverables	76
Host Defenses Performance Matrix and Assured Deliverables	82
Malware Control Performance Matrix and Assured Deliverables	84

MODULE 4 - NETWORK SECURITY MONITORING	87
Network Security Monitoring	89
NSM Deployment	90
SPAN	91
RSPAN (Remote Switch Port Analyzer)	91
NSM Limitations	92
NSM Data Types	93
Full Content Data Analysis	93
Full Content Data Summary Analysis	94
Full Content Data – Individual Packet Analysis	94
Extracted Content Data Analysis	96
Transaction Data Analysis	97
Session Data Analysis	97
Statistical Data Analysis	98
Meta Data Analysis	99
Alert Data	100
NSM Deployment	100
NSM Deployment models	101
Stand-alone NSM	101
Distributed NSM	101

Commonly Used Tools for Building NSM	102
SGUIL	102
SQERT	103
BRO	103
ELSA	104
Xplico	105
Argus	106
SANCP	106
Review Questions	107
MODULE 5 - EVENT SOURCE CATEGORIES AND THE RECOMMENDED USE CASES	111
Event Source Categories and the Recommended Use Cases	113
Anti-Spam	114
Anti-Spam Detection and Processing Techniques	114
Hashing or Checksums	115
Open Relay Checks	115
RBL check	115
Bayesian Filter	116
Heuristic	116
Signatures	116
Black Listing and White Listing	116
Anti-Spam Event Categories	116
Recommended Use Cases and Correlation Rules	117
Antivirus	119
Event Categories	120
Recommended Use Cases and Correlation Rules	121
End-point Threat Protection / Application Control / Whitelisting solution	123
Recommended Use Cases and Correlation Rules	124
Web / Application Server or Database	126
Recommended Use Cases and Correlation Rules	128

Data Loss Prevention / File Integrity Monitor	129
Recommended Use Cases and Correlation Rules	131
Financial Application	135
Recommended Use Cases and Correlation Rules	136
Host Based Firewall	140
Recommended Use Cases and Correlation Rules	141
Single Sign-On Solution	143
Benefits of SSO	144
Recommended Use Cases and Correlation Rules	145
Intrusion Detection/Prevention System	147
Recommended Use Cases and Correlation Rules	148
Network Based Firewall	152
Firewall Technologies	153
Packet Filtering	153
Network Address Translation (NAT)	153
Circuit Level Gateways	154
Application Proxies	154
Virtual Private Network	154
FW Logs - Common Categories	154
Recommended Use Cases and Correlation Rules	155
Network User Behavior Analysis (NUBA)	158
Popular Threat Detection Methodologies used by NUBA	159
Recommended Use Cases and Correlation Rules	159
Operating System	**163**
Recommended Use Cases and Correlation Rules	164
Proxy	**165**
Types of Proxy	166
Event Categories	166
Recommended Use Cases and Correlation Rules	167
Storage	**169**
Recommended Use Cases and Correlation Rules	169

Virtual Private Network	**172**
Recommended Use Cases and Correlation Rules	173
Vulnerability Scanner	**174**
Recommended Use Cases and Correlation Rules	175
Review Questions	**178**
Answers to Review Questions	**181**
Glossary	**186**
Index of Tables	**189**
Index of Figures	**191**

Introduction

Security analytics can be defined as the process of continuously monitoring and analyzing all the activities in your enterprise network to ensure a minimal number of occurrences of security breaches. A Security Analyst is the individual that is qualified to perform the functions necessary to accomplish the security monitoring goals of the organization. This book is intended to improve the ability of a security analyst to perform their day to day work functions in a more professional manner. Deeper knowledge of tools processes and technology is needed for this.

A firm understanding of all the domains of this book is going to be vital in achieving the desired skill set to become a professional security analyst. The goal of this book is to address the problems associated with the content development (use cases and correlation rules) of SIEM deployments.

1. The Security Operation Center Fundamentals domain details the much-needed basics one should know about a Security Operation Center. The key areas of knowledge include:

    - Security Operations Center Fundamentals
    - SOC Challenges
    - Regulatory compliance requirements

- SOC Services
- SOC Roles and Teams
- SOC Topology
- SOC Reports
- In-House SOC vs Outsourced SOC
- Outsourced SOC – Service level agreements
- SOC Analyst – Desired Skill Set
- SOC Roles
- Information Needed by SOC Roles

The ability to understand security operation Tools, Processes, Roles and Responsibilities of SOC professionals are all key elements that go into this domain.

2. SIEM deployment domain addresses the processes and steps involved in selection and deployment of an SIEM solution for the enterprise.

    The key area of knowledge includes:

    - SIEM Selection and Deployment
    - SIEM Tools
    - Types of Reports
    - SOC Metrics
    - How to Select SIEM
    - Collector to source communication Protocol
    - Challenges or Risks in Building a SOC

Proper understanding of processes and technology related to SIEM helps security professionals in designing and deploying security monitoring solutions in a very effective way. The security analyst is responsible for security threat detection to all levels based on the solution they implement.

3. MSSP SLA domain is meant for making a securing analyst understand the means, components and terms of an MSSP SLA through a sample service level agreement. This includes an oversight of the common terms and criteria included in an SLA.

4. The Network Security Monitoring domain focuses on the deeper packet or stream level analysis of data. Network security monitoring is a collection of different publically available tools for the deeper analysis of network traffic. The tools and techniques used for building and operating an NSM internally for your organization is described in detail.

The key areas of knowledge include:

- Network Security Monitoring
- NSM Deployment
- NSM Limitations
- NSM Data Types
- NSM Deployment

- NSM Deployment models
- Commonly used Tools for building NSM

5. The Recommended Use Cases and Correlation Rules domain deals with the selection of proper use cases and correlation rules. The effectiveness of security monitoring is based purely on the strength of deployed use cases and correlation rules. Event sources are categorized in to a number of categories based on their type, and a list of minimum recommended use cases and correlation rules are suggested.

The key areas of knowledge include:

Recommended use cases correlation rules for;

- Anti-spam
- Anti-virus
- End point threat protection/ Application control/whitelisting solution
- Web/Application server or database
- Data loss prevention /File integrity monitor
- Financial application
- Host based firewall
- Single sign on
- IPS/IDS

- Network based firewall
- Network user behavior analysis
- Operating system
- Storage
- VPN
- Vulnerability Scanning solution
- NAC solution

Module 1
Security Operations Center Fundamentals

Why do we need a SOC?

The Security Operations Center plays a significant role in real time detection of threats and post threat response. There are several tools and solutions that are in use in SOC environments. This book will take you through all the must know SOC technologies and tools. The Security Operation Center is the place where all network devices, security solutions, applications and database systems are monitored. SOC also deals with the periodic assessment of threats through the use of vulnerability management tools, network security monitoring solutions, and continuous security monitoring products. End point security management, Incident Response, compliance monitoring etc. are also the other major functions of the Security Operations Center team.

SOC Challenges

There are several challenges in security monitoring, in the following section you will find more details about it.

Amount of Data

SOC tools must have the capability to handle tons of data from disparate systems, platforms, and applications. Security monitoring solutions will be acting as the collection and aggregation points of logs, the huge amount of data collection should not create any performance or throughput issues. Performance issues may directly result in interruption of monitoring services or SLA violations in case of MSSPs. The lack of raw or indexed logs will result in compliance violations. So it is extremely important to select the throughput and efficiency of SOC solutions before selecting and deploying it in your SOC.

Log rate limiting is a common practice security practitioners follow to reduce the amount of logs getting aggregated in SOC collection points, Log managers or SIEM collection points. Log rate limiting polices limit the number of logs generated at the event source itself. This ensures effective utilization of your SIEM's Events Per Second (EPS) based license.

However, rate limiting is not always priority driven. Most of the network security vendors do not offer selective rate limiting. This means you may miss highly critical logs due to the implementation of log rate limiting.

Along with rate limiting, organizations may also have control over the type or class of logs generated by the security systems. For example, Cisco IOS gives an option to selectively generate logs. Example -1 Shows the log rate limiting policy configuration in a Cisco Router.

Example -1

Router#configure terminal
Enter configuration commands, one per line. End with CNTL/Z.
Router(config)#logging host 10.10.11.14
Router(config)#logging rate-limit 20 except warnings
Router(config)#end
Router#

In the above example logging rate-limit configuration command limits the number of syslog packets sent to the syslog server to 20 events per second. In this case, it is a selective rate limiting configuration as the policing is not applicable for "warning" category logs.

Numerous End-points and Billions of Logs

Several sets of network infrastructure and security devices are in place in enterprise networks, all of these products generate logs, moreover thousands of end users get connected to the corporate network over wireless or mobile networks. The present security controls do not count the peer to peer communication between connected wireless or cellular end points. The recent developments in networking like SDN - Software Defined Networking is slowly redefining the infrastructure architecture itself. This brings d for revised Information Security Policy or configuration. Organizations are increasingly using cloud deployed instances or applications, most of these applications are business critical, so are the logs generated by them.

Sophisticated Attacks

It is quite difficult to initially detect the modern day sophisticated attacks just by monitoring, collecting and correlating the logs generated by different end points. Most of the time the characteristics of the threat will be identified only by deep post threat analysis.

For Example, Detection of "Lateral Movements" of an Advanced Persistent Threat (APT), needs cross correlation of multiple logs from different event sources.

Regulatory Compliance Requirements

Compliance standards mandate retention of security data. The log archiving should be in such a way that it is easy for the auditors to go back to logs from previous years to trace security breaches. The type of the security data needed, penalties for non-compliance and the minimum retention period vary per regulations.

No organization will be interested in taking the risk of not retaining logs as per the compliance requirements. Non-compliance may result in huge monetary fines and civil or executive liability, moreover having the organizations name associated with a security breach will affect the trust association it has with the customers and the existence of the business itself.

The below table lists the retention requirements of different compliance standards.

Regulatory Standard	Retention Period
SOX	7
PCI-DSS	1
GLBA	6
EU Data Retention Directive	2
Base II	7
HIPPA	6 or 7
NERC	3
FISMA	3

Table 1 Regulatory / Compliance Standards and Retention Periods

SOC Services

SOC functions seven days a week, 24 hours in a day. Typical services offered by SOC are,

- Continuous Threat monitoring and Incident Detection

- Incident Response
- Threat Mitigation
- Rule/Signature updates
- Threat Intelligence Integration
- Vulnerability Assessment
- Web Application Scanning
- Compliance Monitoring
- Managed Devices

Continuous Threat Monitoring and Incident Detection

Continuous Threat monitoring and Incident Detection - This is achieved with the monitoring of SIM/SIEM consoles, IPS/IDS consoles, AV/AS/UTM consoles and DLP/SIV/Endpoint security consoles.

Incident Response

It includes preliminary incident response, isolation of threats and coordination of different functional teams responsible for threat mitigation. Incident response is one of the major functions of the Security Operations Team.

Threat Mitigation

Most of the time SOC team members play a significant role in threat mitigation, they also do the necessary checks needed to make sure that the vulnerability or loophole is completely eradicated. SOC team members may suggest changes to existing security controls for eradication of threat and may also perform re-evaluation of threat with custom scripts or vulnerability management tools.

Rule/Signature Updates

IPS/IDS, End-point security, and Firewall rules are normally updated by SOC. In some organizations, OS and Application patch management is also performed by the Security Operations Center team. Custom signature development, retuning of the signatures and revoking of signatures in use may also be a function of the Security Operations Center team.

Threat Intelligence Integration

Integration of threat intelligence feeds with existing SIM/SIEM, perimeter security appliances like firewall and content filtering solutions is one of the prime responsibilities of the SOC team. Nowadays many of the organizations are opting for their own Threat Intelligence Platform that can consume feeds from different threat intelligent providers.

The SOC SME is usually responsible for the generalization of the data received from different threat intelligence providers. SOC resources use this intelligence to identify new attacks in time and also for reconfirmation of identified threat.

Constituency

Constituency is a term used in SOC to represent a set of customers to whom SOC provides services, these includes users, sites, information technology assets, clients, partners and organizations. A typical SOC will collect billions of security events every day, the processing power, throughput, storage space needed for the analysis and storage of security events is huge. Committee on Natural Security Systems defines an event as "Any observable occurrence in a system and or network events sometimes provides indications that an incident is occurring."

SOC Roles and Teams

A typical SOC will have multiple levels of teams performing one specific or different tasks.

TIER – 1 team is responsible for real time monitoring of security events and they also attend phone calls from clients or users related to security incidents along with other routine tasks.

The TIER – 1 security monitoring team converts alerts to a CASE based on the default threshold settings and escalate it to TIER -2. Usually the threshold level is defined based on the category and severity of the incidents, criticality of the application or resource involved in, the business impact it may have etc.

Tier-1 team only does the basic analysis of the event and doesn't hold the event with them for more than thirty minutes. Again, the process of escalation will be as per corporate /MSSP SOC escalation policy requirements, expertise of the team members involved. Event volume etc. also plays a significant role in this process. Escalation is done by Tier-1 team also to prevent the chances of missing other relevant security events.

Tier-2 team is responsible for in-depth analysis of the security events. It may take a few hours to even weeks for them to do the deep analysis. There may be multiple levels of teams above Tier-2, the incidents will be escalated to them in order if the situation demands. Tier-2 is also responsible for coordinating the post incident's actions with the constituency. Before involving the constituency, they are supposed to do the necessary checks needed for determining the relevancy of the event. For a relevancy check the Tier-2 team trusts the application / system criticality data (documents with a description of how relevant a particular asset or application is to the organization), the data available from vulnerability management solution, adversary information provided by commercial/open source threat intelligence providers.

Information provided by the partners/manufacturers of the product, history of similar kinds of threats that have happened in the past and other documented data like the response time in Service Level Agreement(SLA) are considered for the process of escalation. Incidents may be associated with hundreds to thousands of security events. Recovery from an incident usually demands participation of internal and external experts. Forensic analysis or malware analysis may be performed based on the nature and behavior of the threat. Proper consumption of Cyber Threat Intelligence (CTA), equips the SOC team to properly define and execute response actions. Centralized monitoring for detection of threats in a timely manner and continuous prevention are the major goals/objectives of the SOC. The properly defined and deployed SOC helps the organization to react to threats in a faster way. In fact, every millisecond is important in identifying and preventing threats before they can cause damage.

Modern day SOC aids computer forensics with not only the centralized collection or aggregation of logs, but by offering a platform that can help computer forensic investigators to perform searches in an effective way. Some of the modern day SOC solutions offer additional tools for reassembly network forensics and session analysis. A properly implemented SOC is very instrumental in achieving a shorter recovery time from attacks.

SOC Topology

Along with the aggregation of security logs collected from different end points, an SOC will also act as the aggregation point for other kinds of data like, Full Packet Captures, session statistics information, flow data and other traces like audit trails produced by different endpoints and network infrastructure security devices.

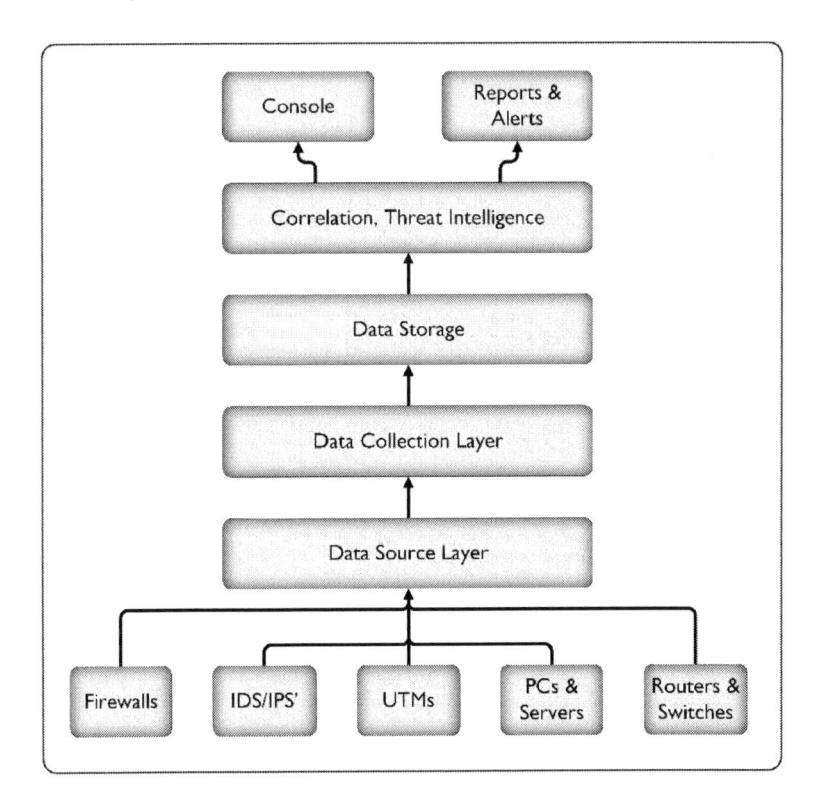

Figure 1 SIM / SIEM Architecture

SOC Reports

SOC solutions offer different kinds of reports targeting different classes of consumers. For example, an executive summary report will only have a brief coverage of the incident plus damage in dollars this incident would have caused to the organizations, or the possible damage it may create if it goes unattended. Such a report is aimed to help the "C" Level team (CSO, CEO, CISO, CTO) to make a quick decision on how to respond to such an event and also to prevent the chances of such an event in future.

The audit and compliance reports offered by Security Monitoring Solutions helps organizations in positioning them in a better way close to the requirements of common regulatory compliance standards. For example, the PCI-DSS Solution pack offered by NETIQ Sentinel offers provision to check all the possible security controls mentioned in PCI-DSS Version-3 standards.

The targeted audience for a technical report produced by SIEM that covers all the aspects of an attack are security analysts and other technical operations team members responsible for mitigation of threats. Such reports may even include recommendations for mitigations, which will help the decision makers in the redefinition of existing security controls or creation of new ones.

In-House SOC vs Outsourced SOC

An organization may opt for Managing, Maintaining and Monitoring the SOC from their premises itself. There are several advantages in setting up an In-House SOC. These include and are not limited to the availability of dedicated technical staff who knows the internal infrastructure of the organization in a better way compared to the MSSP professionals with limited knowledge about the Internal Infrastructure, this helps the SOC analyst in correctly judging the security of an incident.

In-House SOC operations can be tailor made as per the business requirement. The efficiency of an operation of an In-House SOC may be better than MSSP's offering. The major downside of an In-House/Co-operate SOC is the huge initial and periodic investment needed on the Hardware Gear, Storage, Place and Power. There is no way to guarantee the Return of Investment(ROI) in case of an In- House SOC. This makes it extremely difficult to find a compliant security analyst, the chances of building a SOC with the existing resources may be highly risky due to the fact that even seasoned security analyst sometimes miss critical incidents. The chances of collusion between the security analyst and the attacker is increased in the case of an In-House SOC. Not every organization needs its own SOC. The decision to have In-House own SOC should be made with careful analysis.

The factors to consider include:

1. Size/Type of the organization.
2. Number of Incidents reported/noticed in the past.
3. IT budget of the organization.
4. Business/Compliance Requirements

Ready availability of competent SOC analysts having proper expertise in handling different security monitoring solutions and other analysis tools makes an outsourced SOC an attractive option for organizations. Outsourced SOC's are highly scalable and flexible when compared to the In- House offering. Strict SLAs provides finer control of operation and moreover the chances of collusion between the analyst and attacker is minimal. Unbiased decisions and exposure to multiple sets of customers of same segments makes the MSSP security analyst a better choice. The capital retentions associated with an MSSP is less, improper data handling and the storage of the logs off premises brings in additional staff, who know the internal environment, and limited customization options may sometimes make MSSP a less preferred choice.

Outsourced SOC – Service Level Agreements

Response time for different security needs, should be well defined in the SLA. It can range from few hours to even weeks. The top priority, high severity incident, which demands an initial response time of one hour followed by periodic updates every thirty minutes. SLAs may about the escalation and re-prioritization procedures. For example: The priority to security incident may be escalated and converted to priority one incident by the customer. In some cases, the SOC engineer or customer lowers the priority of the incident after the basic analysis of the incident. The procedures/steps to follow in case of an incident, must be well defined in an SLA. Adherence to change management process in case revision of security controls should be considered in SLA. Missing an incident/improper handling of the incident by SOC professional may result penalty. Penalty sometimes may result in termination of the existing contract. Assurance of no reoccurrence of an event, protection against emerging threats and proper effective utilization of Threat Intelligence Data should also be documented. SLAs are meant for improving the quality of the operation, it can be used as a tool by the customer to ensure proper operation of out sourced SOC. The outsourcing contracts normally will include clauses of eventual termination at the end of the contract. The client needs to define and develop a proper exist strategy to ensure smooth transition. The client will plan for either an in house SOC /move to another MSSP provider towards the end of existing contract. This process of transition and associated steps should also be documented. Formal service level metrics are commonly used for measuring the quality of SOC operations. At the end of the contract, if the client is going for an in-house SOC, the existing MSSP partner needs to arrange a number of knowledge transfer sessions Weekly performance reviews verifies the SOC functions. In case of transitioning to an in-house SOC, the MSSP partner will have to work with the internal CIRT team. In some cases, transition is planned phase by phase. For example: The client will only start with, few Tier-2 engineers and all Tier-1 monitoring functions will be handled by the MSSP partner. Once the management has enough confidence the Tier-1 monitoring will also be taken away from the MSSP partner.

The performance review process will analyze:

    A. Response – Make sure that the people who are responding to competent enough to handle the situation.
    B. Reports – The ability of the SOC team to create a different kind of complete SOC reports, that business demands should be checked.

C. Alerts – Make sure that you are getting timely alerts from the MSSP partner on new and in-progress security incidents.
D. Threat Analysis- The threat analysis capabilities of the MSSP team can be measured by taking few sample incidents from the past few weeks.

SOC Analyst – Desired Skill Set

A Security Analyst is expected to have good proficiency in handling different operating systems. Linux is the most commonly used operating system flavor in SOC environments. Majority of the SOC Monitoring solution are built in Linux for configuring data connection from different end points, decent understanding of different features of the operating system is needed. Now Operating Systems offers centralized event log collection. Centralized event log collection needs a server and a number of client (subscriber) computers, more details about windows centralized event configuration can be found at (link). A security analyst must have good expertise on network security devices like intrusion detection system, Intrusion prevention system, firewall, UTM, etc. He also needs to be familiar with directory access protocols like LDAP, database management systems, flat file system storage, various scripting languages, regular expressions, computer forensic tools and information security policy writing. Ethics and integrity are unavoidable qualities of a security monitoring professional. Moreover, he needs to have good reading habits, problem solving skills and management capabilities. A security Analyst needs to be an abstract thinker and he should respond well to very frustrating situations. He should be extremely curious about the final details of an incident. He must be aware of all the low-level details while keeping big picture of situation. It is extremely difficult to find competent SOC analysts, it may few months to locate someone competent enough. Internal knowledge transfers sessions external technology and product training helps SOC analyst to gain the required knowledge. Attrition is a very common issue a SOC. To reduce the rate of attrition, the frequent bonuses, other perks, management opportunities and promotions are given. Companies may sponsor family holiday trips and reduce the stress related issues. Job rotation is also done. SOC is a highly process oriented set of practices. The proper execution SOC needs well defined documentation, that covers all the SOC functions. Ad-hock manner of working is not suitable for a SOC. Pre-defined work flows ensures smooth SOC operations.

SOC Roles

Role	Strategic	Incident Response	Day to Day
CSO	Strategic Advice Metrics Gathering		
Security Manager		Metrics Gathering IR oversight	Metrics Gathering
SOC SME		Issue Triage Investigation	
Security Analyst			Investigations Monitoring & Alerting Device configuration Management Vulnerability Management

Table 2 SOC Roles

Security Analyst

Security Analyst ensures that all the tools deployed in a SOC environment are running optimally. They the monitor the organizational environment continuously for threats, in fact they are front line of security operations most of the time A security analyst will be first point of contact and the interface between different organizational team responsible for mitigation, when a high risk alert or suspected attack begins to affect the business organizations. They are also responsible for the initial phase of forensic investigation.

SME/ Research Specialist

A Security specialist with vast technical expertise and wide experience will be acting as the SME/Research specialist. He will be called on to assist with security incidents that are complex and escalated by other low Tier teams. He normally acts as a consultant to the SOC manager and CISO. The SOC SME is responsible for all kinds of research including things like integration of existing, SOC solutions with threat intelligence feeds, setting up of Network Security Monitoring solutions like Security Onion, STIX/TAXII support etc. SOC SME may be asked to provide POC's (Proof of Concept) on various technical integration requirements. Internal knowledge transfer, review of different vendor products, Revision of existing SOC controls, developing the SOC management frameworks etc. are also the functions of SME.

SOC Manager

SOC Manager translates the Chief Information Security officer's goals and requirements in to set of actions for the SOC team to execute. There will be several issues which needs executive attention or investment. The SOC manager conveys their issues to the CISO and works close with the management to get the necessary approval on budget. The SOC manager acts as an interface between SOC Engineers and CISO. He oversees day to day security operations of the SOC, ensures availability of the resources (people), tools, processes and measurement methods. Talent acquisition is another major responsibility of SOC manager.

Chief Information Security Officer (CISO)

This champion "C" member acts as the primary interface between Security organization and the business owner. He ensures that SOC resources and activities are aligned to the organization business strategy. He is responsible for translating business requirements into security operations objectives. He is expected to educate business executives about how security can enable business innovations. Budget prioritization is another key responsibility of CISO.

Information Needed by SOC Roles

Role	Information Needed
Analysts	• Log and flow data to provide contextual view of security incidents • Alerts which are prioritized based on severity • Access to threat intelligence (TI) feeds • Access to Session analysis, Network forensics & other tools
SOC SME	• Data on emerging threats • End to end and in-depth information on security incidents as they happen to speedup resolution
SOC SME	• Data on SOC resources (staff) management • Up to date status on open security issues
CISO	• Executive summary information on the high priority security risks and incidents. • Overall risk and security posture of the business

Table 3 Information Needed by SOC Roles

Review Questions

1) Overall risk and security posture of the business information is critical for .... work role in security operations center.

    a) L1 security Analyst
    b) SOC manager
    c) Chief Security Officer
    d) Chief Technology officer

2) Access to threat intelligence feeds is recommended for .... work role.

    a) Security Analyst
    b) Chief Security Officer
    c) SOC Manager
    d) HR Manager

3) A properly defined service level agreement should cover .... and ....

    a) Missing or improper handling of SLA
    b) Licensing details of SIEM
    c) Escalation and re prioritization procedure
    d) Assurance of no re-occurrence

4) .... is a term used in SOC to represent a set of customers to whom SOC provide services.

a) Region
b) Clients hub
c) Constituency
d) Village

5) ………. Is responsible for generalization of the data received from different threat intelligence providers.

a) SOC SME
b) SOC Analyst
c) SOC Manager
d) CISM

6) PCI-DSS mandates minimum data retention of …… years.

a) 1
b) 2
c) 3
d) 4

7) HIPA mandates data retention of …… or …… years.

a) 4 or 5
b) 5 or 6
c) 6 or 7
d) 3 or 4

8) Retention of lateral movement of an advanced persistent threat needs ……..

   a) On-site correlation
   b) Remote correlation
   c) Cross correlation
   d) Manual review

9) ………….. In a common practice security practitioner follow to reduce the amount of loss getting aggregated in event sources.

   a) Log rate limiting
   b) Log dumping
   c) Log compression
   d) Log piping

10) ………….. Security monitoring team converts alerts to an incident based in the default threshold settings.

   a) Tier – one
   b) Tier – two
   c) Tier – three
   d) Tier – four

Module 2
SIEM Selection and Deployment

How to Select an SIEM Solution?

An Organization making its first SIEM purchase needs to be well aware of the features offered by SIEM product and also the business requirements. Improper decisions may result in overspending on your SIEM solution. The correctly configured and monitored SIEM solution plays a significant role in identifying security breaches near real time. There are various features and characteristics we need to consider when choosing an SIEM product.

Ease of Deployment

SIEM installation and upgrade should be as smooth as possible. I have personally observed several instances of component upgrade failures in large SIEM deployments, failure of components like event processors/collectors will result in stoppage of data collection for several hours.

Very large MNCs may test the upgrade first in their Lab/QA environment to ensure smooth operations. If the upgrade is successful in the QA environment, then only they will plan for the production set up upgrade. Make sure you verify that the data collection process can be automated. Most of the Modern day SIEM solution offers automatic discovery of data collection endpoints in a production environment. The other factors to consider includes ease of migration of data, support for conversion from standalone SIEM deployments to distributed deployment and availability of the SDK/API or support for custom collectors.

Ease of Data Accessibility

Data should be available both for historical and real time analysis. Sometimes as part of forensic investigations/compliance checks, we may be asked to provide access to the archived data. The time needed for accessing the data should be as minimal as possible. Long term storage of excessive amount of logs may need low compression. Generation of reports that includes historical data demands ready availability of index to perform database queries. The local event database of the SIEM solutions will be used for real time threat analysis. Historic analysis may demand access to the log archive and it is most of the time suitable for an in-depth forensic investigation. SIM solutions offer raw log data storage, which will be useful for forensic analysis.

Provision for Threat Intelligence Integration

Integration of threat intelligence feeds with SIEM improves the response time of detection. The indicators of Compromise information data like IPs,

URLs, File Hashes and Domain Information helps the SIEM user in identifying possible threats without even having correlation rules. The contextual information provided by threat intelligence feeds like history of an IP, Risk scoring provided by the Threat Intelligence Source and TIP- Techniques Tactics and Procedures information helps organization in generation of alerts and post threat investigation. The TIP information provided may be helpful in predicting the nature and behavior of an attack. Proper integration of threat intelligence feeds is useful in defining the response course of action. The threat intelligence data is matched with firewall logs, web proxy logs, net flow information, Other networking device logs and NIDS/NIPS data. Some SIEM vendors produces their own threat intelligence, however most of them now offers customer the provision to integrate multiple threat intelligence feeds in to the SIEM.

In some cases, the SIEM vendor may have their own Threat Intelligence Platform(TIP) that can consume, threat intelligence feeds from both community and commercial providers. The other option is integrating a third-party TIP with the existing SIEM. Threat intelligence is also helpful in validation of correlation rules and relevancy check of a correlation output. Information provided by threat intelligence feeds can be used in reports and alerts as a context for better coverage of threats.

Tools

Your SIEM solution must have integrated tools for converting operational data to actionable information. This tools helps organizations in retracing the actions of the attacker and provides deep insight in to the intrusion activity. Some of the tools are helpful in reassembly and reconstruction of Network streams to its original form. Regular expression can be created and tested from almost all SIEM solutions. Commonly used tracing, editing, searching and capturing tools in Linux environment are available in SIEM CLI. Tools for conversion of event log format, complex reports generations, troubleshooting and debugging, Connectivity issue between connectors and SIEM, disk usage, data migration, manual archiving, scripting etc. are generally expected functions within SIEM products.

Types of Reports

SIEM needs to have capability to generate executive, technical and compliance audit reports as per the business requirements.

SOC Metrics

Event management efficiency of an SIEM should be measured for total raw events, total number of aggregated and analyzed events, total number of correlated events, number of cases opened and initializing of the cases opened. Depending on how many data end points are monitored the amount of raw log data received varies. Additionally, the different types of data collected and the use cases may be considered for measurement of efficiency. The speed of event recognition, event escalation and event resolution is used to calculate the overall response metrics of a SOC.

Further classifications like Per hour / day / week / month, Per security Analyst, Per hour of day/ Per day of week, Case category, Security and number of incidents is also counted in some cases. Effective and efficient service in SOC needs through measurement of people, process and technologies related to security monitoring. Gathered metrics should provide enough information on how well the SOC is operating. The security metrics provides more insight on

- a) Security incidents Trend, is it going up or down?
- b) What is average response time of security operation team on different incidents?
- c) Number of false positions reported
- d) How effective is SOC?
- e) Comparative data on SOC performance with previous month/ quarter/ year information

f) SOC Head count to incident ratio

How to Select SIEM

Selecting a proper SIEM is not an easy task. Before going ahead with the SIEM selection there must be a log review process in place. Log review process needs a corporate logging policy with the details like the review frequency, log retention period, application requirements and compliance requirements. It is important to enable logging on all needed end points. Proper time stamping ensures correct correlation outputs. The collected logs should be stored in a secure way. The log review process identifies abnormal events that need further investigation. To have this first we need to have an idea about the normal event. Organization normally uses a baseline of the events for this detection. Baseline is created with the reference of already captured events. The baseline enlists different kinds of events and categorizes the events which needs investigations.

The enterprise log management policy needs to have specifications about:

1) What all relevant logs needs to be captured?
2) What kinds of events constitute a threat?
3) Response – time for specific kinds of

threat
4) Response – actions that should be taken.
5) How long the events should be retained?
6) Document when the event occurred and response – action taken.
7) Document follow up actions associated with the event.
8) Document this scope of coverage like which assets needs to be included, which assets are internal etc.
9) Document the record of authority(ROA) that covers the log storage location and the retention period of each class of logs.
10) Create an audit trail that covers the follow up of the list of "Events of Interest" and associated actions.
11) Define and document service level agreements.
12) Define and document standard operating procedures.

There are several players offering log management solutions like ArcSight (logger), Loglogic, Sentinel log manager, Splunk etc. Most of these vendors supports both centralized and distributed log collection. The capability of log management solution to pull logs from different end points like databases, Windows, servers should be checked. A majority of end points can forward logs to the log management solution (via Syslog). Syslog by default works with UDP and does not guarantee the delivery of data. However, syslog can be configured to the work over TCP. It is a common practice to secure the communication channel between the log manager / collector and the end-point to avoid confidentiality attacks against sensitive data. The conventional log management solution requires a lot of manual effort for the log review. SIEM addresses this issue with the help of correlation engine. The default "content" offered by SIEM solution is not adequate enough for threat detection in a production environment. Organization define Events of Internet (EOI) and then use correlation rules to generate alerts to overcome this limitation.

Mosaic security offers a comprehensive SIEM vendor comparison tool which helps you to list your requirements and then generate a short-list of vendors. It compares leading vendor products and then creates personalized list of vendors based on your input. The tool is available at Mosaic security research.com/ SIEM- vendor- shortlist- tool. DCIG SIEM appliance offers comparison of nine leading SIEM products. It is available at DCIG.COM/ guides/ 2014-15-SIEM – appliance- buyers- guide. "Evaluation Criteria for security information and event management document" and "SIEM selection tool" created by ANTON CHUVAKIN of Gartner is another wonderful resource that helps customer to select a proper SIEM solution for the environment. Gartner

Magic quadrant for SIEM provides a qualitative analysis of several security analytics products. Gartner usually rates vendors upon two criteria:

1) Completeness of vision
2) Ability to Execute

Gartner places each vendor in one of the four quadrants:

1) Leaders – With highest score on both criteria
2) Challenges – With more score on ability to execute than completeness of vision
3) Visionaries – With lower ability to execute and higher completeness of vision
4) Niche players – With lower ability to execute and completeness of vision

SOC Functional Modules

The five distinct functional modules of an SIEM are:

1) Event Generators
2) Event Collectors
3) Message Database
4) Analysis Engine
5) Reaction Management Software

These modules are normally built as autonomous part

then combined in a logical way to achieve continuous monitoring and threat response.

Event Generators

All monitored systems act as event generators in SOC. These includes firewalls, IPS/IDS, network equipment's OS's, application, vulnerability assessment and risk assessment tools. Events generators can be broadly classified into two categories, event based generators and status based data generators. Event based data generators or sensors produce events based on specific operation performed on the OS application or over the network. A traffic event generated by an IDS/IPS due to the triggering of an existing rule is a typical example of this. Status based data generators (pollers) produce event data as a reaction to an external process. For example, a ping reply message is created upon the receiving of a ping request. Another good example is an SNMP query probe created by an SNMP manager that generates as output on the probed device which will then be passed back to the enquirer.

Network based or host based IDS is the most commonly seen sensor, other content filtering solutions like Firewalls, Routers, as configured with security controls like ACL's, Switching with L2, L3 security Access control features, wireless Access points and controllers, AAA solutions, DLP boxes, Proxy's, honeypots/honey nets system Integrity verification, Application acceleration solutions, Server Load balancers, Email Security gateways, VPN gateways, SSL Multiplexers, Packet sniffers/Lessing solutions etc.

Sensors – Expected Qualities

Ideally a sensor should have the below capabilities:

1) Continuous operation and fault tolerance: sensors must be fault tolerant it should be able to service a crash without losing data.
2) Resist subversion: The sensor should protect itself from compromise, it should be able to monitor itself continuously.
3) Anti-evasion: A sensor must have the capability to detect and prevent evasion attempts.
4) Overhead: The amount of overhead on log management or SIEM solution should be minimal as possible.
5) Configuration and Scalability: Sensors should be configurable and it should support dynamic configurations.

Pollers generate an alert when a specific state is detected. This is done with the help of preconfigured policies. Pollers are commonly used for service status detects and data integrity checking. For example, NMS solutions like OPEN NMS offers service monitoring with ICMP/SNMP (A free demo of open NMS is available at demo.opennms.org).

Event Collectors

Event collectors are responsible for gathering information from different sensors. They act as log aggregation points. Different end-points uses different log formats. Collectors translate the different formats of logs to a standard format. Collectors connect to a data source either directly or indirectly to collect events. SIEM provides different sets of collectors, in some cases you may develop your own collector with the help of instructions given by the vendor.

To get a clear understanding of collector working let us take a look at OSSEC. OSSEC is a comprehensive host based open source IDS solution that can be integrated with most SIM/SIEM products. An OSSEC Server acts as central hub for all OSSEC agents. SIEM collector aggregates the logs forwarded by the OSSC server. Additionally, customer may opt for direct log forwarding from each OSSEC agent instead of OSSEC SERVER.

```
<ossec_config>
 ...

 <syslog_output>
   <server>192.168.4.1</server>
 </syslog_output>

 <syslog_output>
   <level>10</level>
   <server>10.1.1.1</server>
 </syslog_output>

 ...
</ossec_config>
```

Table 4 Sample OSSEC Syslog Configuration

The direct connection method from collector to endpoint can be either with an agent code residing locally or with the help of a native protocol.

Native Protocol Based Direct Connection

Log data either be pushed from the end-point to the collector after the initial configuration of it or in some cases collector must manually request data from endpoint at a regular interval.

Event protocol

With the help of event protocol the event source

communicates with the collector. Some of these protocols support auto configuration and auto discovery. These are a number of event protocols in use.

Let's see different event protocol options in detail:

    a)   API Based: In this method, the collector uses an API to communicate with the source.

    b)   OPSEC API: OPSEC (Open Platform for security) is an open, multivendor security frame work.

Other Technology companies can partner with Checkpoint with their OPSEC API's. Log expert API (LEA) and event Logging API (ELA) are the two reporting and logging API's offered by OPSEC. OPSEC LEA uses procedure calls to retrieve the logs. Basically, OPSEC LEA allows you to export logs to third party servers. It allows real time and historical retrieval of logs from checkpoint devices. OPSEC ELA is used for securely sending information to the Checkpoint SMS (Security Management Server). With OPSEC ELA other applications can log security events in Checkpoint Event Log.

Other technologies companies can partner with checkpoint with their OPSEC (open platform for security) API's. OPSEC is open, multivendor security framework with a lot of partners. These are two reporting and logging API's in OPSEC.

LEA – Log Export API
This can be used for real-time and historical retrieval of logs from checkpoint devices.

ELA – Event Logging API
ELA is used for securely sending information to the checkpoint SMS (security Management Server) with ELA other applications can log security event in the checkpoint event log.

Collector to Source Communication Protocol

API based –MSWMI
With the MSWMI SIEM's can collect the Microsoft windows events and data in an agentless way. Windows Management Instructions (WMI) scripts or applications automates administrative tasks in the Windows environment. In fact, MS WMI is based on WBEM (Web based Enterprises management) an industry standard to develop technology for accessing management information in an enterprise environment.

Representation of systems, applications, network, devices and other managed components in WMI is done with the DMTF's (Distributed Management

Task Force) Common Information Model (CIM), remote management connections in WMI uses DCOM. The use of WMI API for log collection needs firewall configurations accept incoming external communication on port 135 and dynamic ports needed by DCOM. There is no polling interval in MS windows security Event Log Protocol (that use WMI) based log collection. This is because of the fact that SIEM's receives event notifications from OS to identify when the events are available. The maximum EPS supported by this method is limited to 50.

Microsoft Security Event Log Over MSRPC Protocol

Microsoft security Event Log over MSRPC can collect only standard windows events. MSRPC does not support retrieval of non-standard windows logs MSRPC can support up to 100 events per second per host so it is suitable for medium sized windows servers. High event rate systems should use dedicated agents to collect and forward logs. MSRPC uses NTLM v2 Session security, so it is best suited in environments where event payload security is needed.

WinRM

Modern day windows OS' has the ability to collect copies of events from multiple remote components and store them locally. You can specify types of events to collect in the event subscription. Forwarding and collecting computers are needed for this. This is achieved with Windows Remote Management Service (WinRM) and Windows Event Collector (Wecsvc). We need to enable both WinRM and Wecsvc services on all collecting and forwarding computers. There are two different methods you can use for centralized windows event log collection using WinRM.

    i.   **Collector Initiated Event Forwarding /PULL method**

In this method the collector server contacts event sources at regular intervals to determine whether they have logs to transmit. Scalability issues associated with this method limits the use of it in large enterprises environments.

    ii.   **Source Initiated Subscription**

The remote event log sources forward the logs to a collector server in this method, either HTTP or HTTPS can be used for this forwarding. This is a highly scalable and well suitable model for large enterprise environments. There is no need to specify all the event source computers on an event collection like in collector initiated subscription. Additional configuration steps are needed if the collector computer and all event source computers are in different domain.

More details about this can be found at: https://msdn.microsoft.com/en-us/library/windows/desktop/bb870973(v=vs.85).aspx

SDEE

International Computer Security Association(ICSA) has a new model called SDEE (Security Device Event Exchange) for communication of event generated by security devices. SDEE is highly flexible and allows vendors to extend the standard. Cisco Intrusion Detection Event Exchange (CIDEE) specifics the extensions to SDEE. CIDEE is used in Cisco IPS product.

There are two methods for retrieving events using SDEE:

1) An Event Query
2) Event Subscription

Both of these methods uses SSL to query the SDEE server.

Challenges or Risks in Building a SOC

Right from finding the proper set of people to work in SOC to resolving high-end technical issues, there exist numerous risks in the process of building an SOC.

Below are the major types of risks:

1) Humans
2) Processes and Procedures
3) Legacy and Technology
4) Noise
5) Technical

Humans

It is extremely difficult to find proper set of people with right skills to work in SOC environment. SOC works 24/7 in 365 days. So, the analyst needs to have willingness to work in shifts. In case of geographically distributed SOC environments, language is a concern. The SOC manager has a real challenge in managing the resource/availability of 24/7. Other issue is not all people can apply/avail leaves at a time. SOC has to remain open and operational even during yearly company shut down period. Bonuses and other benefits are commonly used methods for keeping the employees motivated. Periodic technical trainings are also provided to make the security analyst competent with the complex work requirements.

Processes and Procedures

Organizations needs to have well defined and documented processes and procedures to ensure smooth operation of SOC. Companies may develop their own SOC management frameworks for this. Monitoring tools may need integration with the requesting system and ticketing system. It is important to clearly mention the procedure of escalation to follow in case of an incident. Optimization of the processes and procedures will happen overtime with the knowledge learned from the previous incidents.

Legacy and Technologies

While picking the SOC solutions, organizations may look for some legacy on the vendor side. Availability of the configuration guides and other aids, the end of support date and end of life dates needs to be noted. Similarly, companies may also do a valuation of the technologies used in vendor products. This includes, things like the indexing and normalization mechanism in use, online and offline storage methods, searching mechanism used, frontend initialization console, types of reports it can generate, effectiveness of correlation engine etc. Some vendors offer a good collection of default correlation tools and built in dashboards. Almost all vendors support customized dashboards. Rather than going for a solution imposed by a marketing and sales team, one needs to properly analyze different verticals of solutions before making the final call.

Noise

The major sources of noise in SOC are; frequent vulnerability scans, Spam solution alerts, Honeypot activity alerts, ACL/Security logging alerts, IDS/IPS alerts and Antivirus, Anti spyware and Malware scan related alerts. However, it is extremely important to collect and analyze all relevant security related events before categorizing them as noise. The noise reduction techniques should not be a cause for missing critical events. Sometimes the integration of threat intelligence feeds (Block listed IT reputed list) and the collection of flow data (Net flow, J flow, S flow) may result in noise.

Technical

The throughput of a SOC solution is normally binded to the events/second. Having a low EPS will result in random early drops of the events. You need to note down that random dropping is not priority driven, meaning you may miss even critical events due to this. Maintaining a secure channel between the endpoint and the collector is not always achievable. The additional efforts needed to create custom correlation tools in the absence of built in tools is huge. Careful planning and continuous monitoring helps organizations to resolve these sorts of issues.

Review Questions

1) ……. generate an alert when a specific state is detected and is used for service status detection and data integrity checking.

   a) Sensor
   b) Serves
   c) Probe
   d) Poller

2) …….. is responsible for gathering information from different sensors

   a) Event collector or aggregator
   b) Event processor
   c) Flow processor
   d) Connector

3) …….. can be used by other application to log security event in checkpoint security management server.

   a) Event log in API
   b) Log export API
   c) SNMP
   d) SYSLOG

4) ………. can be used for real time historical retrieval of logs from checkpoint devices.

a) Event log in API
b) Log export API
c) SNMP
d) SYSLOG

5) SIEM can collect Microsoft windows events data in an agentless way using ……….

a) MSWMI
b) WBEM
c) MSRPC
d) DCOM

6) ……. does not support retrieval of non-standard windows logs.

a) MSRPC
b) MSRBC
c) API
d) SYSLOG

7) In collector initiated event forwarding for centralized windows log collection ………. issues are very common.

a) Scalability
b) Compression
c) Retention
d) Decompression

8) SDEE with an event query or an event subscription uses .... to the query SDEE server.

    a) FTP
    b) SCP
    c) SSH
    d) SSL

9) The throughput of a SOC solution is binded to the ....

    a) EPS
    b) SPF
    c) Latency
    d) Rate limit

10) The speed of event recognition event escalation and .... is used to calculate to overall response matrix of a SOC.

    e) Event resolution
    f) Event suppression
    g) Event reporting
    h) Event hiding

Module 3
Managed Security Services SLA

MSSP Service Level Agreement

There should be well written several level agreements between clients and MSSP for network capacity, availability requirements, contingency planning in case of failure, network outage alerts, restoration, escalation and reporting time.

Responsibility of each party for implementing, operating and maintaining security control or mechanisms that must be applied to existing network services should also be documented. Separate legal policy statements for information classification, information retention, evidence admissibility, testification and prosecution procedures should also be there. SLA normally act as a measurable tool for review and performance of an MSSP contract. Improved operational visibility can be guaranteed with a meaningful SLA with proper object criteria's. MSSP generally offers standard service level agreements. If the customer has specific service level agreement to demand, MSSP may go on a negotiation with the customer to make the demanded SLA fit with their general standards.

It is a very usual practice that the customer may demand an enhanced level of service due to the nature of their business. Sometimes an external consultant will be called in by the client to measure the adherence to SLA and also for proposing revisions to the existing SLA. MSSP should take necessary steps to compartmentalize each of its service clients from all other service clients. Other than the basic performance and availability requirement an SLA should also consider common compliance requirements. KPI's (Key Performance Indicators) acts as observable parameters for the measurement of service processes. Penalties for non-compliance and rewards for exceeding expectations are also part of SLA document. Though SLA can be considered as a process description document it constitutes both legal and financial instruments. Careful planning and proper review should be there while defining an SLA to avoid common ambiguities and misunderstandings.

Assessing an SLA

It is extremely important to analyze the SLA for both customer and MSS provider to ensure:

1) That the SLA provides value to the customer.
2) SLA provides a good margin to the service provider with minimal risk.

The terms in SLA should be defined in a way so a customer can correlate and understand its value with their business model. The operational risk associated with each of the agreed terms must be estimated by the service provider. The impact of a failure to meet an

SLA on both the customer's and the service provider's business should be assessed. The service provider must have a framework or a mechanism which will help a client to measure the progress and current status of an SOC operation. Statistical information in the form of reports or other documentation should be provided to the customer in a pre-agreed interval. Cost effectiveness is another factor to be considered before going ahead with a very strict SLA. An SLA should not have any implicit functions that are undefined and result in ambiguity.

Managed Security Services SLA Sample

Listed below is an example of an SLA between MSSP and a customer. The information given below is meant only for the general understanding for a security practitioner and is not a readymade SLA sample to be used in a production environment.

Managed SIEM Appliance Incident Notifications					
	Type of Incident				
Security Incident	Highly Critical	Critical	High	Medium	Low
Response Time	30 Minutes	45 Minutes	60 Minutes	120 Minutes	4-48 Hours
Commitment	30 Minutes	45 Minutes	60 Minutes	120 Minutes	4-48 Hours

Table 5 Managed SIEM Appliance Incident Notifications

Managed Log Monitoring Incident Notifications

	Type of Incident			
Incident Notification Time Commitment	No logging activity	Unavailability of log sources / Connectivity Issues	Unusual logging rate	Corrupted logging / compliance violations
	30 Minutes	30 Minutes	30 Minutes	30 Minutes

Table 6 Managed Log Monitoring Incident Notifications

Standard changes related to Managed Device/service

	Type of Device				
	Managed UTM	Managed FW, IDS/IPS, NAC, WAF	Managed Vulnerability Scanning	Managed Log Monitoring	Managed SIEM Appliance
Implementation Time		Within XX hours after getting the request with client manager approval	Within XX hours after getting the request with client manager approval	Within XX hours after getting the request with client manager approval	Within XX hours after getting the request with client manager app

Table 7 Standard changes related to Managed Device/service

SIEM Technology Use Cases and Practices

Managed Device/service Outage Notifications

Notification Time Commitment	Managed UTM	Managed FW, IDS/IPS, NAC, WAF	Managed Vulnerability Scanning	Managed Log Monitoring
	20 Minutes	45 Minutes	45 Minutes	45 Minutes

Table 8 Managed Device/service Outage Notifications

Other changes related to Managed Device/service

Type of Device

	Managed UTM	Managed FW, IDS/IPS, NAC, WAF	Managed Vulnerability Scanning	Managed Log Monitoring	Managed SIEM Appliance
Implementation Time		Within XX hours after getting the request with client manager approval	Within XX hours after getting the request with client manager approval	Within XX hours after getting the request with client manager approval	Within XX hours after getting the request with client manager app

Table 9 Other changes related to Managed Device/service

Service Uptime assurance of Managed Device/Service

Response Time	Type of Device				
	Managed UTM	Managed FW, IDS/IPS, NAC, WAF	Managed Vulnerability Scanning	Managed Log Monitoring	Managed SIEM Appliance
	99.99%	99.96%	99.99%	99.80%	99.99%

Table 10 Service Uptime assurance of Managed Device/Service

Managed device replacement notification

Notification Time	Type of Device				
	Managed UTM	Managed FW, IDS/IPS, NAC, WAF	Managed Vulnerability Scanning	Managed Log Monitoring	Managed SIEM Appliance
	At least 72 hours in advance after the change confirmation	At least 72 hours in advance after the change confirmation	At least 72 hours in advance after the change confirmation	At least 72 hours in advance after the change confirmation	At least 72 hours in advance after the change confirmation

Table 11 Managed device replacement notification

Managed Vulnerability Scanning Incident Notifications				
Incident Notification Time Commitment to client from MSSP	Failure to scan	Highly Critical vulnerability that needs immediate attention	High severity vulnerability that needs attention	Medium to Low Vulnerability that needs to be noted
	30 Minutes	30 Minutes	4 hours	8 Hours – 48 Hours

Table 12 Managed Vulnerability Scanning Incident Notifications

Access Control Performance Matrix and Assured Deliverables

Sl. No.	Deliverables	Turnaround Time / Frequency
1	Access failure by prioritized logical grouping (e.g. payment processing resources)	Report once in 7/15/30 days based on the agreed model
2	Top access destinations by users/groups and anomalous access	Report once in 7/15/30 days based on the agreed model

Sl. No.	Deliverables	Turnaround Time / Frequency
3	Access login success and failure (internal); by user, system, by device class, by time (with details)	Report once in 7/15/30 days based on the agreed model
4	Top access failures by source, destination, user, business unit	Report once in 7/15/30 days based on the agreed model
5	Unusual access to prioritized logical grouping (e.g. financial reporting resources)	Within XX minutes of incident declaration by MSSP SOC team
6	Multiple account logons from different geographic locations	Within XX minutes of incident declaration by MSSP SOC team
7	Suspicious access attempts or failure followed by success from same source	Within XX minutes of incident declaration by MSSP SOC team
8	Privileged user access by access failure, by critical resource, by method, by different location/same time	Report once in 7/15/30 days based on agreed model. In case of real time detection of such suspicious event Client management will be informed within XX minutes of incident declaration by MSSP SOC team
9	Top privileged user access follow by configuration changes	Within XX minutes of incident declaration by MSSP SOC team

SIEM Technology Use Cases and Practices

Sl. No.	Deliverables	Turnaround Time / Frequency
10	Administrative changes to directory service user and group objects; by admin, by user, by group, by resource Criticality	Within XX minutes of incident declaration by MSSP SOC team
11	Use of trusted and service accounts, by volume, by time of day, by domain	Report once in 7/15/30 days based on the agreed model
12	User activations, privilege change and terminations by device class	Report once in 7/15/30 days based on agreed model. In case of real time detection of such suspicious event Client management will be informed within XX minutes of incident declaration by MSSP SOC team
13	Remote access login success and failure (VPN, other); by user, by device class, by time with details	Within XX minutes of incident declaration by MSSP SOC team
14	Unusual service account, terminated account use, login success and failures	Report once in 7/15/30 days based on agreed model. In case of real time detection of such suspicious event Client management will be informed within XX minutes of incident declaration by MSSP SOC team

Table 13 Access Control Performance Matrix and Assured Deliverables

Boundary Defenses Performance Matrix and Assured Deliverables

Sl. No.	Deliverables	Turnaround Time/frequency
1	Top access failures by source and destinations	Report once in 7/15/30 days based on the agreed model
2	Top inbound connections to internal sources by system, user, bandwidth and time	Report once in 7/15/30 days based on the agreed model
3	Top outbound connections to external sources by system, user, bandwidth and time	Report once in 7/15/30 days based on the agreed model
4	Top outbound DMZ connections to external sources by system, user, bandwidth and time	Report once in 7/15/30 days based on the agreed model
5	Top perimeter attacks by category	Report once in 7/15/30 days based on the agreed model
6	Top dropped traffic from DMZ, FW	Report once in 7/15/30 days based on the agreed model

Sl. No.	Deliverables	Turnaround Time/frequency
7	Top blocked internal sources by port, by destinations	Report once in 7/15/30 days based on the agreed model
8	Top blocked outbound connections by port, by destination	Report once in 7/15/30 days based on the agreed model
9	Unusual DNS access and requests	Report once in 7/15/30 days based on agreed model. In case of real time detection of such suspicious event Client management will be informed within XX minutes of incident declaration by MSSP SOC team
10	Changes to active and standby configurations by perimeter device class	Report once in 7/15/30 days based on agreed model. In case of real time detection of such suspicious event Client management will be informed within XX minutes of incident declaration by MSSP SOC team
11	Top unusual peak bandwidth utilization sources and destination	Report once in 7/15/30 days based on the agreed model
12	Top bandwidth by protocol, by connection, by source, by destination	Report once in 7/15/30 days based on the agreed model

Sl. No.	Deliverables	Turnaround Time/frequency
13	Configuration changes FW, VPN, WAP, Domain	Report once in 7/15/30 days based on the agreed model
14	Failure FW, VPN, WAP, Domain	Report once in 7/15/30 days based on agreed model. In case of real time detection of such suspicious event Client management will be informed within XX minutes of incident declaration by MSSP SOC team
15	Multiple login failures by FW, VPN, Domain	Report once in 7/15/30 days based on agreed model. In case of real time detection of such suspicious event Client management will be informed within XX minutes of incident declaration by MSSP SOC team
16	Excessive VM movement by VM, by guest host	Report once in 7/15/30 days based on agreed model. In case of real time detection of such suspicious event Client management will be informed within XX minutes of incident declaration by MSSP SOC team
17	Noncompliance VM movement by VM, by guest host	Report once in 7/15/30 days based on agreed model. In case of real time detection of such suspicious event Client management will be informed within XX minutes of incident declaration by MSSP SOC team

Sl. No.	Deliverables	Turnaround Time/frequency
18	Wireless network access by location, by user, by failed attempts	Report once in 7/15/30 days based on the agreed model

Table 14 Boundary Defenses Performance Matrix and Assured Deliverables

Network and System Resource Integrity Performance Matrix and Assured Deliverables

Sl. No.	Deliverables	Turnaround Time/frequency
1	Installation of unauthorized software:	Report once in 7/15/30 days based on agreed model. In case of real time detection of such suspicious event Client management will be informed within XX minutes of incident declaration by MSSP SOC team
2	Configuration changes outside approved changes (maintaining separate change reference data)	Report once in 7/15/30 days based on agreed model. In case of real time detection of such suspicious event Client management will be informed within XX minutes of incident declaration by MSSP SOC team

Sl. No.	Deliverables	Turnaround Time/frequency
3	Top business critical devices with critical resource utilization (memory, processor, storage, fan)	Report once in 7/15/30 days based on the agreed model
4	Top device / system restarts	Report once in 7/15/30 days based on agreed model. In case of real time detection of such suspicious event Client management will be informed within XX minutes of incident declaration by MSSP SOC team
5	Top process start and failure (filtered)	Report once in 7/15/30 days based on the agreed model
6	Object access denied	Report once in 7/15/30 days based on agreed model. In case of real time detection of such suspicious event Client management will be informed within XX minutes of incident declaration by MSSP SOC team
7	DNS configuration changes	Report once in 7/15/30 days based on agreed model. In case of real time detection of such suspicious event Client management will be informed within XX minutes of incident declaration by MSSP SOC team

Sl. No.	Deliverables	Turnaround Time/frequency
8	DNS faults	Report once in 7/15/30 days based on agreed model. In case of real time detection of such suspicious event Client management will be informed within XX minutes of incident declaration by MSSP SOC team
9	Account changes by critical resource	Report once in 7/15/30 days based on agreed model. In case of real time detection of such suspicious event Client management will be informed within XX minutes of incident declaration by MSSP SOC team
10	Excessive VM movement by VM, by guest host	Report once in 7/15/30 days based on agreed model. In case of real time detection of such suspicious event Client management will be informed within XX minutes of incident declaration by MSSP SOC team
11	Top critical system/device changes per user, per device class, per IT services	Report once in 7/15/30 days based on the agreed model
12	Unauthorized changes, by criticality, as percentage and trend	Report once in 7/15/30 days based on the agreed model

Sl. No.	Deliverables	Turnaround Time/frequency
13	Changes to configurations by device class, by user, by criticality	Report once in 7/15/30 days based on the agreed model
14	Systems outside configuration standards; by criticality, class, business unit, ratio and trend	Report once in 7/15/30 days based on the agreed model
15	Percent of systems without approved patches	Report once in 7/15/30 days based on the agreed model
16	Top attacks by exploited vulnerable systems	Report once in 7/15/30 days based on the agreed model
17	Top inbound and outbound connections by system, user, bandwidth and time Unusual scanner / probe activities	Report once in 7/15/30 days based on the agreed model
18	Nonstandard port activity	Report once in 7/15/30 days based on agreed model. In case of real time detection of such suspicious event Client management will be informed within XX minutes of incident declaration by MSSP SOC team

Sl. No.	Deliverables	Turnaround Time/frequency
19	Actual and suspected systems with Peer:2:Peer software or communications	Report once in 7/15/30 days based on agreed model. In case of real time detection of such suspicious event Client management will be informed within XX minutes of incident declaration by MSSP SOC team
20	Top system issue/incident by incident category	Report once in 7/15/30 days based on the agreed model
21	Noncompliance VM movement by VM, by guest host	Report once in 7/15/30 days based on agreed model. In case of real time detection of such suspicious event Client management will be informed within XX minutes of incident declaration by MSSP SOC team
22	High resource utilization by VM guest host, by resource types	Report once in 7/15/30 days based on agreed model. In case of real time detection of such suspicious event Client management will be informed within XX minutes of incident declaration by MSSP SOC team

Sl. No.	Deliverables	Turnaround Time/frequency
23	Devices with unauthorized or anomalous communications (SMTP, etc.)	Report once in 7/15/30 days based on agreed model. In case of real time detection of such suspicious event Client management will be informed within XX minutes of incident declaration by MSSP SOC team
24	Vulnerability to incident ratio and open/closed vulnerability trends	Report once in 7/15/30 days based on the agreed model
25	Attacks against vulnerable systems classified by criticality	Report once in 7/15/30 days based on the agreed model
26	Device/device group availability percentage	Report once in 7/15/30 days based on the agreed model
27	Failed backup services (or other similar services) by system, by time, by business unit/service	Report once in 7/15/30 days based on agreed model. In case of real time detection of such suspicious event Client management will be informed within XX minutes of incident declaration by MSSP SOC team

Table 15 Network and System Resource Integrity Performance Matrix and Assured Deliverables

Host Defenses Performance Matrix and Assured Deliverables

Sl. No.	Deliverables	Turnaround Time/ Frequency
1	IPS/IDS events classified as incidents by network, by service	Report once in 7/15/30 days based on the agreed model
2	Top incidents by attack type, by source, by destination	Report once in 7/15/30 days based on the agreed model
3	Top attack sources and destinations by volume or destination criticality	Report once in 7/15/30 days based on the agreed model
4	Attacks identified and resolved	Report once in 7/15/30 days based on the agreed model
5	Top traffic by source by application, by source type, by business unit	Report once in 7/15/30 days based on the agreed model
6	Unauthorized and suspicious network traffic by source, by destination, by type	Report once in 7/15/30 days based on the agreed model

Sl. No.	Deliverables	Turnaround Time/ Frequency
7	H Suspicious behaviour by source, by destination, by type	Report once in 7/15/30 days based on the agreed model
8	Suspicious communications by source, by destination, by type	Report once in 7/15/30 days based on the agreed model
9	Attack investigation open and close ratio and trends	Report once in 7/15/30 days based on agreed model. In case of real time detection of such suspicious event Client management will be informed within XX minutes of incident declaration by MSSP SOC team
10	Wireless IDS alerts	Report once in 7/15/30 days based on agreed model. In case of real time detection of such suspicious event Client management will be informed within XX minutes of incident declaration by MSSP SOC team

Table 16 Host Defenses Performance Matrix and Assured Deliverables

Malware Control Performance Matrix and Assured Deliverables

Sl. No	Deliverables	Turnaround Time/Frequency
1	Top reported malware threats	Report once in 7/15/30 days based on the agreed model
2	Anti-virus trends; prevented, detected, remediated	Report once in 7/15/30 days based on the agreed model
3	Spam trends; identified and removed	Report once in 7/15/30 days based on the agreed model
4	Top malware attacked sources, and by prior vulnerability issues	Report once in 7/15/30 days based on the agreed model
5	Top unusual traffic to and from sources	Report once in 7/15/30 days based on the agreed model
6	Top source and destinations of malicious connections	Report once in 7/15/30 days based on the agreed model
7	Top systems with multiple infections / top systems re-infected	Report once in 7/15/30 days based on the agreed model
8	Top systems with suspicious malware activity	Report once in 7/15/30 days based on the agreed model

Sl. No	Deliverables	Turnaround Time/Frequency
9	Anomalous network activity	Report once in 7/15/30 days based on agreed model. In case of real time detection of such suspicious event Client management will be informed within XX minutes of incident declaration by MSSP SOC team
10	Atypical email or web communications	Report once in 7/15/30 days based on agreed model. In case of real time detection of such suspicious event Client management will be informed within XX minutes of incident declaration by MSSP SOC team
11	Atypical port/application use	Report once in 7/15/30 days based on agreed model. In case of real time detection of such suspicious event Client management will be informed within XX minutes of incident declaration by MSSP SOC team
12	Anti-virus stop, start, update failures	Statistical report once in 7/15/30 days as agreed and notification of update failures and signature parsing issues within 30 minutes of incident declaration by MSSP SOC team.

Table 17 Malware Control Performance Matrix and Assured Deliverables

SIEM Technology Use Cases and Practices

Module 4
Network Security Monitoring

Network Security Monitoring

Network Security Monitoring provides meaningful data for intrusion analysis in the shortest amount of time. NSM is the comprehensive collection of data to ease the process of analysis to detect and respond into intrusions. Todd Heberlein developed network security monitoring in 1998, it was a kind of intrusion detection system that used live or offline network traffic as its input. In 1993 Air force Computer Emergency Responds Team (AFCERT) with the help of Heberlein developed Automated Security Insuring Measurement System(ASIMS). Most of the modern-day organizations build their own Computer Incident Respond Team (CIRT).

CIRT team members use NSM:

   i. To collect and aggregate all network derived data.
  ii. To analyze the captured network data to identify intrusions or intrusion attempts.
 iii. To define the response strategy, in case of an attack.
  iv. To perform forensic analysis and risk or damage analysis.

NSM is not responsible for directly preventing intrusions, but it will help the organization to identify the attempts and prevent the objectives of adversaries. Data provided by the NSM is very useful in predicting the objectives of an attacker. It is in fact quite difficult to detect data exfiltration attempts by using conventional security solutions.

Network Security Monitoring and Continuous Security Monitoring are not the same thing. NSM focuses on adversaries and CSM is based on vulnerabilities. Continuous Security Monitoring alone cannot give you sufficient protection from all threats. The good part is NSM helps organizations to contain the activities of adversaries before they complete their mission.

Security platforms like intrusion Prevention System, Content Filtering Solution, Antivirus etc. focuses on blocking or denying the attack from happening. NSM can be used for providing better visibility of different phases of an attack.

NSM Deployment

The CIRT team with the help of the network infrastructure management engineers configures layer 2 switches to export copies of the traffic to the NSM server. The NSM server needs to have all the software needed for traffic analysis. It may not be practically possible to collect all the network traffic from all available switches. Moreover, doing so may result in duplicate collection of data at NSM server so it is important to properly identify the switches on which the exporting feature has to be enabled. Some organizations may opt for dedicated hardware based network taps instead of configuring the switches for exporting the data. There are number of companies offering different hardware tapping solutions to achieve this.

SPAN

Switch Port Analyzer (SPAN) can be used for exporting the network traffic from a switch if both NSM mirrored port is on the same switch.

Below example shows how to set up a SPAN session for monitoring source port traffic to a destination port in a Cisco switch.

```
Switch(config)# no monitor session 1
Switch(config)# monitor session 1 source interface fastEthernet0/1
Switch(config)# monitor session 1 destination interface fastEthernet0/10 encapsulation dot1q
Switch(config)# end
```

RSPAN (Remote Switch Port Analyzer)

RSPAN is used in scenarios where the NSM is located at a different switch port than the monitoring switch port.

Below example shows how to configure a RSPAN session to monitor multiple source interfaces, and configure the destination RSPAN VLAN and the reflector-port in source and destination Cisco switches.

Source Switch

Switch(config)# monitor session 1 source interface fastEthernet0/10 tx
Switch(config)# monitor session 1 source interface fastEthernet0/2 rx
Switch(config)# monitor session 1 source interface fastEthernet0/3 rx
Switch(config)# monitor session 1 source interface port-channel 102 rx
Switch(config)# monitor session 1 destination remote vlan 901 reflector-port fastEthernet0/1
Switch(config)# end

Destination Switch

Switch(config)# monitor session 1 source remote vlan 901
Switch(config)# monitor session 1 destination interface fastEthernet0/5
Switch(config)# end

NSM Limitations

Network security Monitoring is a difficult to implement task in the case of enterprise wireless networks. Wireless end hosts communicate with each other in an encrypted way. This makes NSM ineffective however, this is applicable only in the case of node to node wireless communication. If a wireless host accesses the internet or any other corporate website this traffic has to traverse through the enterprise network.

If mobile hosts are using cellular networks within enterprise environment you may need to get necessary legal approval before tapping the data.

NSM Data Types

Network Security Monitoring deals with or captures different kinds of data. These include:

- Full Content Data
- Extracted Content Data
- Transaction Data
- Session Data
- Statistical Data
- Meta Data
- Alert Data

Full Content Data Analysis

Full content data is the exact copy of a network traffic.

The security analyst can perform two major types of analysis with this kind of data.

Full Content Data Summary Analysis

In this type of analysis security analyst looks into summary of the captured data. This is generally done by looking into the header details of the packets. The below example shows the use of Tcpdump tool for summary data analysis.

Full Content Data – Individual Packet Analysis

In this security analyst picks some sample packets out of the whole captured data and then performs a full inspection of it. Hexadecimal and ASCII representation of the packets will be used for analysis, from L2 to L7 (payload) command line tools like "tcpdump" or GUI tools like "Wireshark" can be used for this kind of analysis.

The below example shows the use of Tcpdump tool

```
# tcpdump -nnvvXSs 1514 -c 2
tcpdump: data link type PKTAP
tcpdump: listening on pktap, link-type PKTAP (Packet Tap),
capture size 1514 bytes
17:58:39.128544 IP (tos 0x0, ttl 64, id 48715, offset 0, flags
[DF], proto TCP (6), length 76)
    192.168.1.4.63423 > 188.172.192.5.5938: Flags [P.],
cksum 0x0b1d (correct), seq 2586084325:2586084349,
ack 3333128064, win 4130, options [nop,nop,TS val
262368849 ecr 566659564], length 24
        0x0000:  3c1e 0434 0a13 a099 9b15 943f 0800
4500  <..4.......?..E.
        0x0010:  004c be4b 4000 4006 3e02 c0a8 0104
bcac  .L.K@.@.>.......
        0x0020:  c005 f7bf 1732 9a24 83e5 c6ab 7f80 8018
.....2.$........
        0x0030:  1022 0b1d 0000 0101 080a 0fa3 6e51
21c6  ."..........nQ!.
        0x0040:  89ec 1130 1b00 0000 0000 0f00 0000
1200  ...0............
        0x0050:  0000 1b00 0000 1800 0000             ..........
17:58:39.554518 IP (tos 0x0, ttl 116, id 24523, offset 0,
flags [DF], proto TCP (6), length 76)
    188.172.192.5.5938 > 192.168.1.4.63423: Flags [P.],
cksum 0x1ca3 (correct), seq 3333128064:3333128088, ack
2586084349, win 515, options [nop,nop,TS val 566664557
ecr 262368849], length 24
        0x0000:  a099 9b15 943f 3c1e 0434 0a13 0800
4500  .....?<..4....E.
        0x0010:  004c 5fcb 4000 7406 6882 bcac c005 c0a8
.L_.@.t.h.......
        0x0020:  0104 1732 f7bf c6ab 7f80 9a24 83fd 8018
...2.......$....
```

Extracted Content Data Analysis

Extracted content data analysis focuses on high level stream content rather than the MAC, IP and protocol headers. Videos, images, other files etc. exchanged between computers can be analyzed in detail through this method.

Extracted content data analysis sometimes needs reconstructions or reassembly of streams. Xplico is an open source tool which can be used for this reconstruction of session.

Below screenshot shows the reassembly of a mms page using Xplico.

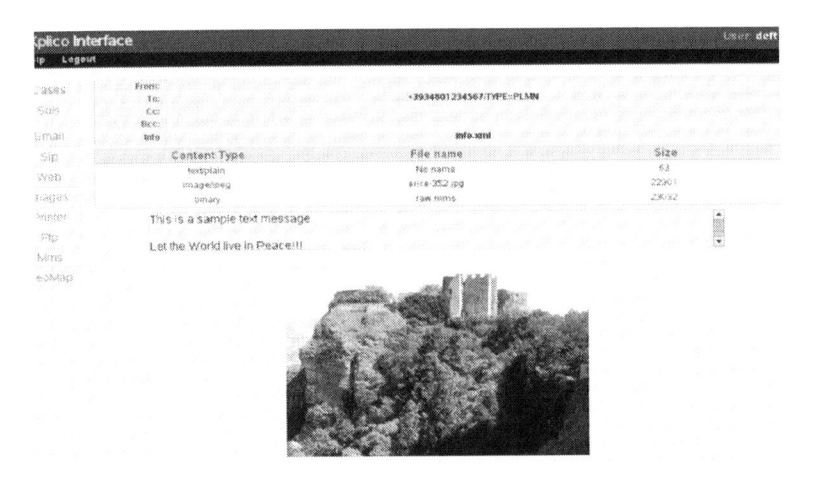

Figure 2 Xplico Interface

Transaction Data Analysis

Transaction data analysis focuses on requests and responses exchanged between endpoints. For example, a legitimate HTTP session will have GET requests followed by a 200 OK or not found response messages. If you are finding HTTP POST without an associated HTTP GET it may be an indication of a data exfiltration attempt using HTTP POST. Network Security Monitoring uses tools like Bro for transaction data analysis.

Session Data Analysis

Session data is the complete end to end communication record between two end hosts. Transaction data is only a subset of session data with details like Source Address, Destination Address, Source Port, Destination port, Session start time, Session end time, amount of bytes or data transferred, protocols used and timestamp.

Open source tools like Bro and Sguil are commonly used for this kind of analysis.

Bro Alerts

Security Operation Center – Analyst Guide

```
CaptureLoss::Too_Much_Loss              SSH::Password_Guessing
Conn::Ack_Above_Hole                    SSH::Watched_Country_Login
Conn::Content_Gap                       SSL::Certificate_Expired
Conn::Retransmission_Inconsistency      SSL::Certificate_Expires_Soon
DNS::External_Name                      SSL::Certificate_Not_Valid_Yet
FTP::Bruteforcing                       SSL::Invalid_Server_Cert
FTP::Site_Exec_Success                  Scan::Address_Scan
HTTP::SQL_Injection_Attacker            Scan::Port_Scan
HTTP::SQL_Injection_Victim              Signatures::Count_Signature
Intel::Notice                           Signatures::Multiple_Sig_Responders
PacketFilter::Dropped_Packets           Signatures::Multiple_Signatures
ProtocolDetector::Protocol_Found        Signatures::Sensitive_Signature
ProtocolDetector::Server_Found          Software::Software_Version_Change
SMTP::Blocklist_Blocked_Host            Software::Vulnerable_Version
SMTP::Blocklist_Error_Message           TeamCymruMalwareHashRegistry::Match
SMTP::Suspicious_Origination            Traceroute::Detected
SSH::Interesting_Hostname_Login         Weird::Activity
SSH::Login_By_Password_Guesser
```

Figure 3 Bro Alerts

Sguil Session data analysis output

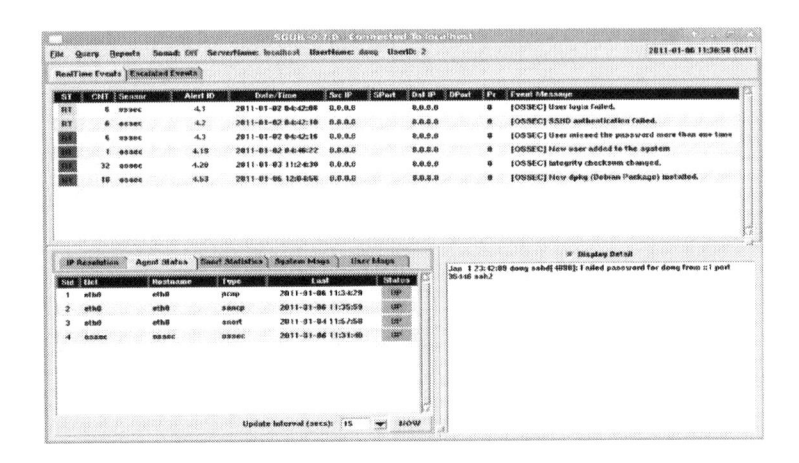

Figure 4 Sguil Session data analysis output

Argus is another nice tool which can be used for session data analysis.

Statistical Data Analysis

SIEM Technology Use Cases and Practices   98

As the name implies this kind of analysis focuses on the statistical information like file /data size, start and end time of transfer etc. Wireshark or Capinfos (bundled with Wireshark) can be used for this kind of analysis. Wireshark offers different kinds of statistical data information.

Wireshark endpoint statistics

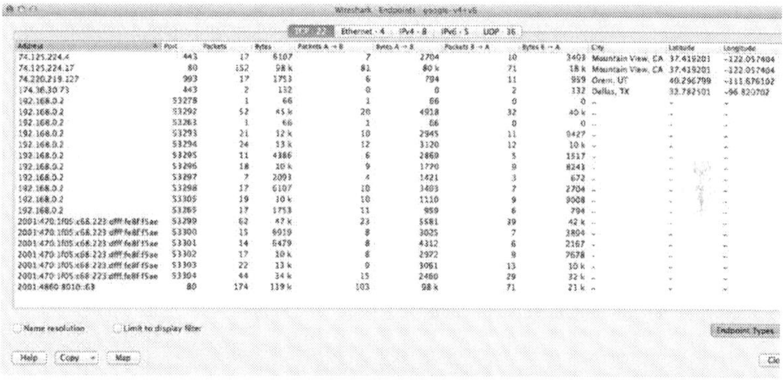

Figure 5 Wireshark endpoint statistics

Meta Data Analysis

Data about data is known as metadata. External tools or resources like whois, ip2config, robotex.com etc. are used for meta data analysis. IP reputation lookup and other kind of threat intelligence information is also useful for this analysis.

Alert Data

Intrusion detection systems triggers events when they interpret data traffic. The events generated by security Appliances upon devices of matching condition is called Alert. Snort and Suricata are the two most commonly used open source solution.

Snort and Sguil are used for alert data analysis.

NSM Deployment

Organizations must decide on the type of network traffic they need to monitor before going ahead with NSM. A thorough analysis of network traffic needs to be performed to identify the placement locations of NSM sensors. An NSM server can be either a commercially available appliance or something we build on your own.

There may be multiple monitoring interfaces in an NSM server. It is a fairly good idea to allocate one or more CPU core per monitoring interface. A basic deployment of NSM needs a bare minimum of 8GB RAM. There should be adequate space available for the storage of the network traffic and other NSM data. Normally RAID is used in storage.

NSM Deployment models

NSM Deployment can be either, standalone or Distributed.

Stand-alone NSM

In a standalone NSM deployment a single NSM instance acts as sensor and server. This model is suitable for small and medium based companies. Typically, it is used in scenarios where there is only one segment is being monitored. All the functions of the NSM like monitoring analysis and reporting is performed by one single box.

Distributed NSM

An all in one box approach is not suitable for very large and complicated enterprise network environments. We need to segment the process of collection, analysis and reporting separately to make the NSM scalable for this kind of requirements. Multiple sensors placed at different locations collect and interpret traffic and then forwards the collected data to the NSM server. Distributed models can monitor multiple network segments effectively.

Commonly Used Tools for Building NSM

NSM is a collection of different open source tools for advanced threat analysis. The commonly used tools include and not limited to:

- SGUIL
- SQERT
- BRO
- ELSA
- Xplico
- Argus
- SANCP

SGUIL

It uses a number of tools for its different functions. MySQL 4.x/5.x is used as the back-end storage mechanism. The intrusion detection engine uses either SNORT/SURICATA. IDS alert decoding is done with the help of Berniyard or Berniyard-2. TCP IP session recording is with the SANCP. OS fingerprinting tool used is p0f. TCPdump and Wireshark are used for session and packet analysis.

SQERT

SQERT is a simple web application, that is used to query the SGUIL backend database. The visual frontend of the SQERT provides contextual information like Metadata, Grouped Result sets, Time series representations etc.

SQERT instruction image and a demo is available at: http://github.com/int13h/SQERT

BRO

BRO is basically an advanced traffic analyzer, that can analyze all traffic for signs of suspicious activities. BRO provides different sets of log files that carries information about network activity in detail. The application layer details like HTTP URI's, MIME types, DNS responses, SMTP session details etc. are very useful in advanced traffic analysis. BRO by default provides binary extraction from http sessions. The extracted binary files can be further analyzed with the help of external tools. The other functions offered by BRO includes Malware detection, Vulnerable software detection, Brute-Force attack detection and SSL certificate validation. BRO is very customizable and extensible.

The Heart of BRO is an Event Engine that converts packet streams (Network Streams) into a series of higher level events. The events are derived in such a way that it will represent the network activity in a policy neutral way. The policy script interpreter executes, Event handlers and extracts properties from the events.

ELSA

Enterprise Log Search and Archive (ELSA) provides a fully asynchronous web based query interface, that will help the security analyst to search for any arbitrary strings from billions of stored records. The framework used is based on Syslog-NG, the backend storage is with MySQL and full text search functionality is provided by Phinx.

The records can be either logs or alerts. A single instance of ELSA can receive and index more than 30K events per seconds. It supports active directory/LDAP integration for authentication and authorization. For highly scalable requirements distributed architecture with clusters is recommended. ELSA is capable of generating Ad-hock reports/graphs based on arbitrary queries even on very large data sets. ELSA uses Google Visualization for dashboards. Normalization is by default available for CISCO logs, SNORT/SURICATA, BRO, SNARE etc.

Xplico

Xplico is an advanced network forensic analysis tool, that supports reconstruction of data with the ability to recognize the different protocols with a method called PIPI (Port Independent Protocol Identification). Xplico can extract content like images, files, cookies, videos etc. from web sessions. It is also very useful in email analysis, as it supports reconstruction of IMAP, POP and SMTP protocol data. The other protocol Xplico can reconstructed are VOIP, MSN IRC HTTP and FTP.

Xplico System Architecture

There are Four major components in Xplico system architecture:

1. Dema
2. Xplico
3. Data Manipulators
4. Visualization Systems

Dema (Decoding Manager) is responsible for:

a) Input data handling
b) Manage configurations and History files for the decoder and the manipulators.
c) Launch the decoders and the manipulators
d) Control the execution of decoders and

Manipulators

The Xplico decoder reads the raw data from capture dissector block and then forwards it to the protocol dissector's block. Finally, the dispatcher block handles re-organization of the reconstructed and normalized data or sends it to manipulator as needed.

Argus

Argus is a powerful real time flow monitor, that offers comprehensive data network traffic auditing. Argus reports are suitable for historical and near real-time processing for forensics trends and alarm/alerting. Argus can read packets directly from network interface and classify it into network transactions.

You can find more details about Argus at:
http://qosient.com/argus

SANCP

SANCP (Security Analyst Network Connection Profiler) is commonly used for statistical network traffic analysis. SANCP is capable of creating connection logs and record network traffic for the purpose of auditing, historical analysis, and network activity discovery.

Review Questions

1) .... is recommended for exporting of logs if both NSM and monitoring port are in same switch.

    a) SPAN
    b) RSPAN
    c) FSPAN
    d) MSPAN

2) .... is recommended for exporting of logs if both NSM and monitoring port are in two different switches.

    a) SPAN
    e) RSPAN
    f) FSPAN
    g) MSPAN

3) …….. is commonly used for meta data analysis.

    a) WHOIS
    b) ARP
    c) NETSTAT
    d) DD

4) …….. is used to query SGUIL database backend.

    a) SQUERT

b) SQLTI
c) SQUERY
d) SNORBY

5) ……… is an event engine that converts packet streams into series of higher level events.

a) BRO
b) BRI
c) PRO
d) PRI

6) ……… is a powerful real time flow monitor, that offers comprehensive data network auditing.

a) ARGUS
b) PRI
c) BRI
d) PRO

7) …….. is commonly used for statistical network statistics analysis.

a) SANCP
b) ARGUS
c) PRI
d) PRO

8) ……. can read packets directly from network interface and classify it into network transactions.

a) ARGUS
b) PRO
c) BRI
d) Wireshark

9) …….. focuses on high level stream analysis and can be used for analysis of video, image and other files exchanged between computers.

a) Extracted contest data analysis
b) Summary analysis
c) Packet decoding
d) DPI

10) ……. focuses on requests and responses exchanged between end points.

a) Transaction data analysis
b) Argus
c) Wireshark
d) TCPDUMP

Module 5
Event Source Categories and the Recommended Use Cases

Event Source Categories and the Recommended Use Cases

The guidelines provided in this module helps SOC professionals in understanding and responding to security monitoring requirements in a more professional manner. Additionally, the use cases and correlation rules proposed in this module aids in making the security monitoring service more relevant to the threat landscape. The use cases recommended are for the event source category.

The major event source categories considered are -

- Anti-spam
- Anti-virus
- End-point threat protection/Application control/whitelisting solution
- Web/Application server or database
- Data loss prevention /File integrity monitor
- Financial application
- Host based firewall
- Single sign on
- IPS/IDS
- Network based firewall
- Network user behavior analysis
- Operating system
- Storage

- VPN
- Vulnerability Scanning solution
- NAC solution

Anti-Spam

There are several solutions like gateway based filters, client side applications and mail server integrated solutions for anti-spam. The gateway filters are dedicated anti-spam solutions that are often coupled with anti-virus to provide an end to end mail filtering service.

Gateway filters off-load the performance and bandwidth consumption issues of running them on the mail server directly. Mail servers integrated anti-spam solutions run on the server directly processes the spam inline. Client side application that runs on end user's system directly to process spam is not widely-used solutions in a corporate environment. However, the heuristic capabilities of these solutions and lower pricing makes it the perfect choice for a home user.

Anti-Spam Detection and Processing Techniques

Anti-spam solutions use different techniques for the detection and processing of spam. These includes and not limited to:

1. Hashing or checksums
2. Open relay checks
3. RBL check
4. Bayesian filter
5. Heuristic
6. Signatures
7. Black listing and white listing

Hashing or Checksums

Hash values of specific portion of the spam emails is computed and stored in the anti-spam solutions. An email that matches the stored hash will be flagged as spam.

Open Relay Checks

Open relay checks verify whether source mail server permit relays. Mail servers that are configured to relay can be misconfigured by the attacker to limit problem with SPAM black listing. Anti-spam solutions block email from source servers that permits relaying.

RBL check

Malicious Anti-spam solutions may use the real time black lists for blocking spam emails.

Bayesian Filter

Bayesian filters uses user input for calculating the statistical probability an email spam.

Heuristic

The probability of spam is calculated statistically by the combination of a variety of detection mechanism to recognize specific patterns that indicates spam.

Signatures

Specific keywords within a message are checked for the identification of spam.

Black Listing and White Listing

In black listing the anti-spam solution blocks messages from a specific user defined source address, domain or IP. Anti-spam solutions can also be configured to permit messages from user defined white list only.

Anti-Spam Event Categories

As a security analyst one should consider developing and implementing at least the below set of recommended use cases and correlation rules for an anti-spam event source.

Below are the major event source categories to be considered from security perspective.

- Email spam
- Instant messaging spam
- Comment spam
- Junk FAX (Out of Scope for Security Analytics)
- Internet telephony spam
- Unsolicited text messages (Out of Scope for Security Analytics)

Recommended Use Cases and Correlation Rules

Sl. No.	Use Case	Event Type/ Category	Correlation Rule
1	Trigger alert for the EMAIL SPAM originated from inside host.	General Email SPAM	ATYPICAL/ UNUSUAL outbound Email, possible SPAM

Sl. No.	Use Case	Event Type/ Category	Correlation Rule
2	Trigger alert for SPAM in the incoming Email with RBL , IP reputation & MIME header checks.	General Email SPAM	ATYPICAL/UNUSUAL inbound Email, possible SPAM TOP SPAM sources reported
3	Trigger Alarm if Phishing content is found in an email	General Email SPAM	PHISHING content inside email , possible spear phishing attempt/ SPAM
4	Trigger Alarm if SPAM content is found in an IM flow	Instant messaging spam	ATYPICAL/ UNUSUAL Instant messaging communication detected, possible SPAM
5	Trigger Alarm if SPAM content is found in a VOIP flow	Internet Telephony SPAM	ATYPICAL/ UNUSUAL Internet Telephony communication detected, possible SPAM

Table 18 Recommended Use Cases and Correlation Rules

Antivirus

Anti-malware software helps in the prevention, detection and removal of malicious software. The modern-day antivirus programs are capable of providing protection against malicious browser help objects (BHO), key loggers, backdoors, Trojans, rootkits, worms, adware, spyware, spam, phishing attacks, APT, privacy threats and DDOS attacks.

The common detection method incudes:

- Sand boxing – Behavioral-based detection by allowing the program execution in a sandboxed environment and capturing all its actions.

- Data mining – Data mining and machine learning algorithms classify the behavior of a file (as either malicious or benign) given a series of file features that are extracted from the file itself.

- Signature based detection – Compares the suspected file or pattern with its signature database to detect known threats.

- Heuristics – Compares the suspected files or pattern with the generic signature specific to a Virus Family.

- Behavioral-based – Detection based on the behavioral pattern of the malware.

- Root kit detection - A combination of advanced detection techniques is used for this.

Event Categories

The three major categories of events to be considered from an Antivirus event source for effective security monitoring are –

1. AV Definition / Signature Database Status events – Helps the Security Analyst detect the state of protection and virus and spyware signature definitions updates.
2. Scan - antivirus scan related events.
3. Treatment –events related to the action done to the infected files.

Recommended Use Cases and Correlation Rules

Sl. No.	Use Case	Event Type	Correlation Rule
1	To monitor antivirus software logs to track if detected viruses are cleaned properly.	AV Scan	Failed AV mitigation or cleaning detected, possible persistent virus infection.
2	Identify machines that are not updated to the latest AV definitions.	AV Update	Detect unprotected end points, possible Antivirus disable attempt. Detect Anti-virus stop, start, update failures.
3	Identify machines that are updated to the latest AV definitions.	AV Update	Report of the Current AV protection Posture
4	Identify quarantine action failed events.	AV Scan	Report of Anti-virus trends; prevented, detected, remediated

Sl. No.	Use Case	Event Type	Correlation Rule
5	To monitor access requests to fixed-function end-point devices, such as point-of-sale (POS), medical equipment, Industrial control systems, SCADA, aeronautical system & to prevent unauthorized access attempts.	PoS	Detect unauthorized access attempts to fixed-functions in end points
6	To perform user / Administrator activity monitoring & to ensure compliance.	UAM	Detect unusual user activity
7	Identify events where the user chose to delete an item.	AV-Treatment	Track forced file removal events.
8	Identify events where the user chose to ignore an item.	AV-Treatment	Report AV recommended action bypass attempts.
9	Identify events of the applications that were quarantined and restored.	AV-Treatment	Detect failed quarantine-restore attempts.

Table 19 Recommended Use Cases and Correlation Rules

End-point Threat Protection / Application Control / Whitelisting solution

End-point security monitoring tools are used for prevention and detection of threats against the devices which they are running on. Though the threat visibility of the attack is limited the end-point devices communicate with its server to share information about the data. So, this makes it important to monitor end-point security server and client event data. SIEM boxes should have policies to correlate activities on end points servers and clients.

Application white listing solutions allows the execution of specific application based on defined policies related to users, groups, systems and other attributes. The trust worthiness of an application can be determined by verifying the software vendors trusted certificates or with the path value used by the applications. Legitimacy of an application can also be checked with the hash values of files affiliated with an application using common hashing protocols.

Behavior analytics also plays a considerable role in the detection of rogue applications. It is not easy to define generic use cases for this kind of event sources. The features offered by the solutions should be analyzed case by case for developing effective use cases.

Recommended Use Cases and Correlation Rules

Sl. No.	Use Case	Event Type	Correlation
1	To identify & prevent the use of unauthorized software in enterprise environment. Detect the malicious software implantation, propagation, scanning & intrusion nearly real time.	Rogue Software	Installation of unauthorized software and the use of rogue applications
2	Detect & prevent zero day attack initiation & progress in enterprise environment nearly real time.	Zero Day	Detect possible zero day attack initiation.
3	To identify the data access attempts & to prevent the data loss by strict monitoring of files, directories, USB's & other removable devices.	External devices	Detect possible data exfiltration attempts. Top and unusual Web and database application access.

Sl. No.	Use Case	Event Type	Correlation
4	Detect & prevent malicious software infection / propagation from USB's & other removable devices.	External devices	Detect unauthorized removable device in use
5	To monitor access requests to fixed-function end-point devices, such as point-of-sale (POS), medical equipment, Industrial control systems, SCADA, aeronautical system & to prevent unauthorized access attempts.	PoS	Detect unauthorized access attempts to fixed-functions in end points
6	To perform user / Administrator activity monitoring & to ensure compliance.	UAM	Detect unusual user activity

Sl. No.	Use Case	Event Type	Correlation
7	To perform malware impact assessment to aid investigation with details like time & type of attack, mode of propagation, which endpoints have been infected and which machines are engaged in suspicious activity.	Impact Assessment	Detect suspicious end point activity

Table 20 End-point threat protection / Application control / Whitelisting solution - Recommended Use Cases and Correlation Rules

Web / Application Server or Database

Enterprises use web applications for quick, user friendly and effortless access to cooperate data. Most of the time applications are installed on top of common web server solutions like IIS or Apache. These servers may be laden with vulnerabilities and should be patched and monitored to avoid security risks. Attackers use specially crafted SQL, LDAP and other commands to access web application server database content. Though secure coding practices like strict input validation, exception management, data encoding and data escaping helps to minimize the threats web application server is exposed to, it is crucial to capture and report each possible attack.

Integration of database access monitoring (DAM) application to SIEM is a prevalent best practice now. All database transactions are captured and alerts are generated for possible policy violation attempts. Sensitive data access monitoring is enabled near real time by this.

# Recommended Use Cases and Correlation Rules

Sl. No.	Use Case	Event Type	Correlation
1	Monitor web server and web middleware application logs to detect ATYPICAL events.	Database Activity	Web application attacks per server and application. Web application attacks remediated. Top web application attack by type, by source, by destination. Web application attacks not remediated. Web and database platform configuration changes. Web and database platform outages due to configuration changes. Application platform resource utilization anomalies. Database application security issues / trends. Database queries, inserts or deletes that are Atypical. Excessive denied requests by web application by source/ destination. Web application errors by application type. Top Critical SQL commands by administrator. Top monitored database table attribute changes. Top and unusual Web and database application access. Top Web application administrative changes. Top or Unusual application process or resource utilization by application server. Web application outages associated with attacks or configuration changes.

Table 21 Web/Application Server or Database - Recommended Use Cases and Correlation Rules

Data Loss Prevention / File Integrity Monitor

Data exfiltration attempts can be identified and prevented with DLP solutions. Network security teams are struggling with DLP solutions integrated with SIEM, the underlying problem is "attempt to manage SIEM and DLP "separately without seeing them as products part of the "securing monitoring" process. DLP prevent end users from uploading sensitive corporate information to internet through email, cloud storage and other applications. Proper data classification is very much needed for the working of DLP. It is always a fair best practice to review the data classification and alert settings of your DLP before integrating it with your SIEM. This practice will help you to prevent problems with the false alerts generated by DLP. The combination of SIEM and DLP helps organizations in implementing effective security monitoring for compliance violation detection. It helps organizations understand and manage the data that is used, stored and transmitted. It is also useful for PCI-DSS monitoring. By integrating DLP with SIEM organizations can have security analytics in one program. It is also critical to tune your SIEM to focus on where the data is found, doing so helps the network security team responsible for managing the infrastructure protect the sensitive data at the source, in transit and at its destination. SIEM can also play a major role in alerting the DLP about new sensitive resources and the threat to organizations. Improved visibility and control is one of the immediate benefits of integrating SIEM with DLP. Regulatory compliance standards like PCI, SOX, HIPA, GLBA etc. demands confidential information and intellectual property protection and detection of such breaches.

A DLP solutions can detect different kinds of data losses like:

1) Unintentional data leakage by an internal employee.
2) Intentional data theft by an internal employee.
3) Determined data theft by skilled internal employees, external hackers and advanced persist threats or malware.

A DLP system should be capable of dealing with all the three stage of data:

1) Data in use (end points)
2) Data in motion (network)
3) Data in rest (storage)

Data stored in end points can be exfilterated via USB, email, webmail, http, instant messenger, FTP etc. The data in motion exfiltration can be through SMTP, FTP, HTTP etc. The data at rest could be accessed or owned by a wrong person or can reside at a completely wrong place. A DLP mechanism for data in use or data in motion may monitor data flows from sources like a user, an end-point, an email address or a group of them to destinations like an end-point, an email address or a group of them through channels like USB, email or network protocol.

For data exfiltration detection of data at rest a DLP solution may install a discovery agent locally. For this you may need to specify what is sensitive data and the authorized sources to handle it.

Recommended Use Cases and Correlation Rules

Sl. No.	Use Case	Event type	Correlation Rule
1	To determine where data is stored across endpoints and servers. To identify true data owners and detect unusual activities. To monitor Customer Data in transit through & off the corporate network.	Data	Detect possible data exfiltration attempt. Potential sensitive data disclosure. Violations by category

Sl. No.	Use Case	Event type	Correlation Rule
2	To monitor sensitive Intellectual Property data in transit through & off the corporate network. To monitor sensitive Corporate Data in transit through & off the corporate network.	Data	Detect Intellectual Property exfiltration attempt.
3	To monitor changes to the sensitive data in storage.	Data	Detect possible data corruption attempt.
4	Detect policy violations related to the transmission of sensitive data.	Data	Detect possible data exfiltration attempt.
5	Detect sensitive data sent over IPV6.	Data	Detect possible data exfiltration attempt.

Sl. No.	Use Case	Event type	Correlation Rule
6	Detect in-motion data leakage over the web and through email, with DLP policy rules that include content, context, and destination.	Policies	Detect possible data exfiltration attempt.
7	To analyse events related to encryption & decryption of backup tapes and other storage devices.	Confidentiality	Detect possible data confidentiality violation attempt.
8	To identify unauthorized physical or network access, malware, end-user actions that may result in data loss.	Threats	Detect possible data exfiltration attempt.

Sl. No.	Use Case	Event type	Correlation Rule
9	To analyse DLP end-point policy enforcements to prevent information leak.	Data	Detect possible data exfiltration attempt. System Access outside business hours. Top Resource access failure per user.
10	To analyse security events reported on copying of data to removable storage devices and media.	Data	Detect possible data exfiltration attempt. Top users with DLP incidents.

Table 22 Data Loss Prevention / File Integrity Monitor - Recommended Use Cases and Correlation Rules

Financial Application

Modern day SIEM solutions offer seemingly less application monitoring of financial systems. Some financial application like Cleartouch from FISERV collect customer data such as credit and debit card numbers and bank PINs. Moreover, such applications centralize the business actions and allow multiple departments access to the data. Employees who have access to this kind of data only need a fraction of it for their work functions. Knowing exactly who is doing what with this kind of data is critical for preventing security breaches.

Some of the financial service applications collect PII (Personal Identifiable Information) like social security number, mobile number etc. In order to avoid possible mishaps with such sensitive information, a company should monitor the use of it. Organizations use dedicated privilege user application monitoring solutions to monitor their internal storage activities related to financial applications. Integrating PUM (Privileged User Activity Monitoring) with SIEM helps organizations ensure the security and confidentially of customer records and offers protection against all anticipated threats to the integrity of such records and minimizes the inconvenience to the customer.

Recommended Use Cases and Correlation Rules

Sl. No.	Use Case	Event Type	Correlation Rule
1	To ensure that Secure Sockets Layer (SSL) is in use for all sensitive web application data access requests related to procurement, purchasing, making payment, Customer Orders, Order fulfilment and receiving payment from Customers.	Confidentiality	Detect sensitive data transfer over unsecure communication channel.
2	To ensure that all the common end-point protection tools are there in place & is in a properly protected state.	Controls	Detect current end point security posture.

Sl. No.	Use Case	Event Type	Correlation Rule
3	To ensure that operating attack surface on all clients and servers accessing critical financial systems are reduced.	Attack	Detect intrusion attempts on financial applications.
4	To analyse the databases monitoring events and auditing software events reported by financial & accounting applications.	Monitoring	Detect unusual application access attempts. Administrative access to Critical system outside normal business hours.
5	To analyse user log-on/logoff reports (log-in/log-out monitoring) of financial and accounting applications.	User	Detect unusual application access attempts.

Sl. No.	Use Case	Event Type	Correlation Rule
6	To analyse the Log-on Failure Reports of financial & accounting applications.	User Access	Detect unusual application access attempts.
7	To analyse the Audit Logs Access events to financial & accounting applications.	User Access	Detect unusual application access attempts
8	Identify when an object like File, Directory, etc. related to financial & accounting applications is accessed, the type of access (RO/RW) and whether or not access was successful/failed, and who performed the action.	User Access	Detect unusual application access attempts

Sl. No.	Use Case	Event Type	Correlation Rule
9	Analyse local system processes such as system start up and shutdown and changes to the system time or audit log.	System	Detect unusual application access attempts.
10	Analyse event logs for changes in the security configuration settings such as adding or removing a global or local group, adding or removing members from a global or local group, etc.	System	Detect unusual application access attempts.
11	To analyse the status of internal controls in place for accessing financial & accounting applications.	Controls	Detect unusual application access attempts. Unusual access using service account credentials.

Table 23 Financial Application

Host Based Firewall

Host based firewall are designed for protection against security threats originating from LAN environments and can help mitigate the risks of an end-point host. Host based firewall are also known as personal firewalls. The host based firewalls are software modules installed on each individual end-point systems. Most of the personal firewalls offer protection beyond capabilities of a network firewall. It protects end points system from Trojans, spywares and other malicious software. it is typically useful for roaming end users who cannot always be connected to the internet through a hardware firewall. Most of the modern-day operating system comes with integrated personal firewall. However, we cannot expect rich features of a commercial personal firewall from this. Personal firewalls are not a replacement for antivirus solutions. Zone Alarm, Tiny personal firewall, KERIO etc. are examples of commonly used personal firewall solutions.

A well configured personal firewall provides effective protection against different kinds of attacks. Continuously monitoring the personal firewall logs with security monitoring solutions like SIEM is a good idea to detect potential compromises in end-point machines. The internal firewall rules configured in personal firewalls acts as a simple access control list with logging capability. Port scanning activities and malicious software implementation can be identified near real time with the integration of personal firewall with SIEM.

Event Categories

1) Antivirus – Most of the Host based firewalls has AV capabilities.
2) IDS/IPS – Host based Firewalls use IDS/IPS engines for deep inspection.
3) Phishing - Protects the end users from going to phishing websites.
4) Intrusion - Protects end systems from targeted attacks.
5) Data - Monitors data in transit & prevents the malicious data transfer.

Recommended Use Cases and Correlation Rules

Sl. No.	Use Cases	Event Type	Correlation Rule
1	All Antivirus Use Cases.	AV	All AV correlation rules.
2	All Intrusion Detection/Prevention System Use Cases.	IDS/IPS	All IDS/IPS correlation rules.

Sl. No.	Use Cases	Event Type	Correlation Rule
3	Identify the phishing sites accessed by the end user.	Phishing	Suspicious web communication, possible PHISHING attempt.
4	Detect targeted attacks from local networks & internet.	Intrusion	Targeted attack detected.
5	To monitor the system for real-time program activity and connection status.	System	Top System connections.
6	To identify "calling home" attempts by malware for transmitting sensitive data to hackers.	Data	Top source and destinations of malicious connections. Detect C & C communication in progress.
7	To identify attempts to modify critical system & application files.	Data	Critical file access, possible data corruption or exfiltration attempt.

Sl. No.	Use Cases	Event Type	Correlation Rule
8	To identify the user attempts for privilege escalation.	System	Detect Privilege escalation attempts possible system intrusion. Authentication failures by privileged user
9	To identify the attempts for service status modification by processes/users.	System	Service modification request, possible Rootkit implantation
10	Identify the request by application for attributes associated with the processing environment.	System	Reconnaissance or possible information gathering attempt

Table 24 Host Based Firewall - Recommended Use Cases and Correlation Rules

Single Sign-On Solution

Single Sign On (SSO) permits a user to access all the computer resources where he has access permission through a single process of authentication. SSO reduces the human error and inconvenience issues caused by typing in the user credential multiple times. SSO is a difficult to implement technology. Novell's SSO solution works slight different than other SSO solutions. They store the separate user names and passwords of different applications in a common store called SecretStore. Solutions like Open-AM SSO uses HTTP cookies to track user actions. Single Sign On permits to terminate user access to multiple software application with a single action of sign-out.

Benefits of SSO

1) Reduced errors and operating failures.
2) Improved security with a single user authentication.
3) Reduced administrative efforts in managing user accounts.
4) Consistent and reliable performance.

Though there are multiple benefits with single sign on it is important to note down that an SSO solution is a very attractive target for a hacker to perform denial of service attacks. SSO is an expensive retrofit solution to an existing application. The single point of failure nature and the risk associated with unattended end user system that uses SSO should also be considered while designing the integrated monitoring solution with SSO.

Recommended Use Cases and Correlation Rules

Sl. No.	Use Case	Event Type	Correlation Rule
1	To identify & analyse the Auto-provisioning of user accounts by IM solution & to verify the privilege level assigned to each.	Auto-provisioning	Suspicious user account provisioning or modifications.
2	To identify & analyse the Auto-deactivation of user accounts by IM solution.	Auto-deactivation	Suspicious user account deactivations or modifications.
3	To analyse the Identity-synchronization events reported by IM solution.	Identity-synchronization	Suspicious user account attribute changes
4	To verify & analyse the self-service requests events reported by IM solution.	self-service requests	Suspicious user account service requests.

Sl. No.	Use Case	Event Type	Correlation Rule
5	To verify analyse the modification of users & entitlements reported by IM solution.	Delegated- administration	Suspicious user account modifications.
6	To analyse propagation of changes from one system to other.	propagation of changes	Track propagation of user account changes.
7	To analyse user requests for change of their own or others' profiles and requests for additional access rights.	Profiles	Suspicious User Profile modifications.
8	To analyse automatic discovery and classification of systems and accounts by IM solution.	Discovery	Detect rogue system & user accounts
9	To verify the orphaned accounts.	Orphan	Report unused or Orphaned accounts

Sl. No.	Use Case	Event Type	Correlation Rule
10	To verify the privileges assigned to each user by IM solution.	inappropriate privileges	Track inappropriate privileges assignments.
11	To verify the multiple privileges assigned to user accounts by IM solution.	Privilege	Violation of separation of duties.
12	To analyse the Duplication of information Identity information stored in IM solutions.	Duplication	Identity data duplication.
13	To verify & analyse the single sign-on events reported by IM solution.	SSO	ATYPICAL SSO incidents.

Table 25 Single Sign-On Solution - Recommended Use Cases and Correlation Rules

Intrusion Detection/Prevention System

The basic difference between IDS and IPS is the fact

that IDS focuses only on detection and IPS can take actions along with the detection. IDS can passively monitor more than one segment and can monitor traffic that an IPS would never see. IPS actions include drop, reset, shun or custom actions, and it is placed in line with the traffic for taking this action. The "fail open" feature of IPS allows traffic to pass through in case of IPS engine or scan failure. Modern day firewalls come with software modules or hardware daughter cards for IPS/IDS feature. UTM boxes will also have IPS/IDS features in built. For effective security monitoring of firewall events the below set of use cases are recommended.

Recommended Use Cases and Correlation Rules

Sl. No.	Use Case	Event Type	Correlation Rule
1	To identify attacks targeting vulnerabilities in operating systems and applications.	Vulnerabilities	Known vulnerability exploitation attempt

Sl. No.	Use Case	Event Type	Correlation Rule
2	Detect botnet events used to perform targeted Denial of Service (DoS) attacks or steal personally identifiable information (PII)	DOS/PII	PII data ex-filtration
3	Detect both known and unknown threats by comparing the behaviour with the predefined rule set. Detect incidents by comparing traffic patterns that the IPS considers "normal" with new traffic patterns, and deciding whether new traffic patterns fall within acceptable patterns or not.	Rules	Suspicious or unusual incidents

Sl. No.	Use Case	Event Type	Correlation Rule
4	To identify ineffective IPS rule or signature that results in False Positive alarms/actions. To identify ineffective IPS rule or signature that results in False Negative alarms/actions.		Top False Alarms
5	To identify worms that exploit a vulnerability to install itself, scans the network for additional potential victims and self-propagate from one computer to the next.		Worm Outbreaks
6	To identify Trojan's that propagate itself from system to system with human intervention.	Trojans	Trojan propagation
7	To identify buffer overflow attacks against applications & systems.	DOS	Dos or Buffer overflows

Sl. No.	Use Case	Event Type	Correlation Rule
8	To identify scanning, fingerprinting & enumeration attempts against the corporate network or resources by attackers.	Scan	Unusual scanner / probe activities
9	To identify spywares that tracks sites visited with a browser, records keystrokes and mouse clicks & change browser settings to obtain information from computers.	Spyware	User activity monitoring & data capturing by spyware
10	Detect phishing attempts where scammer sends large quantities of genuine-looking e-mail messages to intended victims in an effort to entice them to open an attachment or click a URL.	Phishing	Email Spear Phishing attempts

Sl. No.	Use Case	Event Type	Correlation Rule
11	Detect SYN Floods and Denial of Service (DoS) Attacks against corporate resources.	DOS	DoS Attacks
12	To identify the obfuscation attempts by attacker.	EVASION	Obfuscation/Evasion attempt
13	To identify the tunnelled & encrypted malicious data transfer.	EVASION	Data exfiltration over secure channels
14	To identify the attackers attempt to send malicious network packets in smaller fragments.	EVASION	Fragmented data Exfiltration attempt
15	To identify the attackers attempt to send malicious network packets as protocol specific data.	EVASION	Suspicious protocol traffic

Table 26 Intrusion Detection/Prevention System - Recommended Use Cases and Correlation Rules

Network Based Firewall

Firewall is an access control device which decides which traffic to forward and which traffic not to forward, based on the pre-defined rules. Firewalls screen both inbound and outbound network traffic.

The major features of an enterprise grade network firewall include:

1) Blocking the incoming traffic based on source or destination IP or port.
2) Blocking the outgoing traffic based on source or destination IP or port.
3) Screen network traffic for unacceptable and inappropriate content.
4) Enable remote access of resources.
5) Allow connection to internal network.
6) Generates alerts on network activities.

Firewall Technologies
Packet Filtering

Packet filtering works at the network layer of OSI model. The filtering is based on service type, port number, interface number, source /destination address etc.

Network Address Translation (NAT)

Network address translation (NAT) enables mapping of internal private IP address to external public IP addresses. A firewall can perform one to one or many to one static or dynamic mapping.

Circuit Level Gateways

These are firewall which works under session layer of OSI model. Multiple parameters like address, DNS name, Directory name etc. are used for allowing or denying network access.

Application Proxies

It works as a proxy server that intercepts information passing through the gateway and thus does not allow direct communication. Application proxies will allow a limited number of applications like FTP, SMTP etc.

Virtual Private Network

Most of the modern-day network firewalls act as VPN termination points. This kind of firewall support both site to site and remote access virtual private network connection.

FW Logs - Common Categories

1. Firewall change management Logs
2. Firewall bandwidth monitoring alerts

3. Firewall Internet / Intranet Usage alerts (Permitted and Blocked)
4. Firewall IPSEC/SSL/Tunnel/Point to Point

Recommended Use Cases and Correlation Rules

Sl. No.	Use Cases	Event Type	Correlation Rules
1	Get a complete trail of all the changes done to firewall configuration. Identify 'who' made 'what' changes, 'when' and 'why' to firewall configuration. Identify attempts to start or stop auditing service of the Firewall. Identify attempts to clear trace contents from audit log container.	Firewall change management Logs. Modification of FW audit logging service. Enable FW audit logging service. Disable FW audit logging service. Delete audit records in FW	Changes to active and standby Firewall configuration. Detect Configuration change related to firewall policies and VPN. Detect Audit Log removal attempts

Security Operation Center – Analyst Guide

Sl. No.	Use Cases	Event Type	Correlation Rules
2	Monitor network traffic and generate alert notifications upon sudden spikes in bandwidth. Analyse which user, protocol group or network activity is consuming more bandwidth. Analyse the firewall logs to identify the users violating the corporate internet download/usage policy. Monitoring internet usage (overuse or misuse) by employees. Identify the protocol wise internet usage by the users. Identify the user attempts to access restricted sites. Analyse the firewall logs to identify that which VOIP phones are trying to connect to the VoIP server using TFTP to get the configurations. Detect DoS attack against the application servers by analysing the no of inbound connections to the server farm through firewall. Analyse incoming and outgoing traffic/bandwidth patterns in enterprise network. Identify top Web users, and top websites accessed	FW - Traffic and Bandwidth monitoring events FW - Internet / Intranet Usage alerts.	Top unusual peak bandwidth utilization sources and destinations Top bandwidth by protocol, by connection, by source and by destination Top blocked internal sources by port, by destinations Top perimeter attacks by category Top dropped traffic from DMZ, FW Top blocked outbound connections by port, by destination Unusual DNS access and requests Changes to active and standby configurations by perimeter device class Daily or weekly alerts on top 10 connections from sites of concerns

SIEM Technology Use Cases and Practices

Sl. No.	Use Cases	Event Type	Correlation Rules
4	Identify the VPN tunnel creation by the FW / VPN gateway Identify the VPN tunnel termination by the FW / VPN gateway or user. Generate alerts for file download over VPN session. Generate alerts for object/resource access over VPN session. Identify the bytes of data transferred over VPN session.	IPSEC/SSL VPN or TUNNEL initiation. IPSEC/SSL VPN or TUNNEL termination. IPSEC/SSL VPN or TUNNEL termination due to policy violation, compliance or communication issues Data transfer over IPSEC/SSL VPN or TUNNEL sessions Object/resource binding by any of the participating peer with the other over IPSEC/SSL VPN or TUNNEL sessions Release of the Object/resource binded by any of the participating peer with the other over IPSEC/SSL VPN or TUNNEL sessions Queries regarding the objects / resource access over VPN session.	

Table 27 Network Based Firewall - Recommended Use Cases and Correlation Rules

Network User Behavior Analysis (NUBA)

NUBA offers passive monitoring of user behavior without major network reconfiguration. Continuous real time view of user activities across enterprise network is captured and monitored by the solution. The user role information in your existing directories will be used as the reference for the analysis. Some of these solutions are capable of even controlling user access based on the findings. A centralized active login data base needs to be accessible by NUBA for analysis. If needed LDAP queries will be used for verifying user or group mission. Port mirroring or passive network taps are used by the network user behavior analysis tools for deep packet inspection. Flow data like Cisco netflow, Juniper jflow etc. are used for analyzing changes made by the end users. Event data generated by network user behavior analysis tools are exported to security information event manager (SIEM) either by using SNMP, SMTP or any other protocols. Some of the NUBA tools support importing of vulnerability assessment data for relevancy check of the findings.

Popular Threat Detection Methodologies used by NUBA

Payload Anomaly Detection
Protocol Anomaly: MAC Spoofing

Protocol Anomaly: IP Spoofing
Protocol Anomaly: TCP/UDP Fanout
Protocol Anomaly: IP Fanout
Protocol Anomaly: Duplicate IP
Protocol Anomaly: Duplicate MAC
Virus Detection
Bandwidth Anomaly Detection
Connection Rate Detection

Recommended Use Cases and Correlation Rules

Sl. No.	Use Case	Event Type	Correlation Rule
1	To analyse business user behaviour and activity across the network environment.	UBA	Suspicious behaviour by source, by destination, by type
2	To analyse the environment for network usage, critical assets & to identify malfunctioning devices and detect trends	Statistics	Suspicious communication by source, by destination, by type

Sl. No.	Use Case	Event Type	Correlation Rule
3	To analyse application usage statistics, host-level audit trails or network activity, spam detection and application failure notifications.	Statistics	
4	To compare the internal behavioural analysis data with the one from perimeter devices.		
5	Detect & analyse network and security issues of specific users.	UBA	
6	To perform trend analysis of user activity with the historical behavioural data collected.	UBA	

Sl. No.	Use Case	Event Type	Correlation Rule
7	To detect and analyse Network scans, Service probes, Protocol anomalies, Network behaviour anomalies, Application behaviour anomalies, Unauthorized services detected, Unauthorized communication channels detected, Custom signature deployments & Regular and on-demand signature updates.	UBA	
8	Detect evasive threats with deep packet inspection of protocols like DHCP, AIM, DNS, FTP, HTTP, IRC, Kerberos, POP, SIP, SMTP, SSL, TLS etc.	DPI	Suspicious communications by Protocol

Sl. No.	Use Case	Event Type	Correlation Rule
9	Detect different kinds of unknown and highly customized attacks like - Zero-Day attacks – detection of zero-day attack symptoms Data leakage– misused HTTP(S), FTP, SMB Tunnelled traffic– ICMP, DNS, SSH. Protocol anomalies– detecting changes of use of common protocols and their characteristics. Mascaraed brute-force attack (dictionary, brute-force) Breach of internal security rules by employees.	Threats	Suspicious communications by Protocol

Table 28 Network User Behavior Analysis (NUBA) - Recommended Use Cases and Correlation Rules

Operating System

Almost all the SIEM solutions can receive log data directly from windows, Linux, UNIX, OSX and other operating systems. Dedicated agents like SNARE, Adaptive Log Exporter, Sentinel UNIX agent etc. are also used for exporting logs.

Modern day windows operating system offers centralized windows event log collection. This innovative server subscriber model reduces the complexity of integrating all event sources separately to SIM or SIEM. SIEM providers may offer agents or add-ons for exporting archived windows event logs. Microsoft windows management instrumentation (WMI) API can be used for remote agent less windows event log collection from windows server version 2003, 2008, Windows XP, Windows Vista and Windows 7. Windows event log protocol needs proper configuration of server DCOM settings.

Recommended Use Cases and Correlation Rules

Sl. No.	Use Cases	Event Type	Correlation Rule
Linux/Unix Common OS Logs			
1	To analyse general message and system related events which needs attention.	System	Detect unusual OS incidents
	To analyze OS authentication logs (Successful & Failed).	Auth	
	To analyze kernel level logs for system Panic / failure conditions.	Kernel	
	To analyze scheduled, running & cancelled cron jobs.	CRON	
	To analyse system mail server logs.	MAIL	
	To analyse Apache access and error logs.	HTTPD	
	To analyse OS boot log.	BOOT	
	To analyse Lighttpd access and error logs.	Lighttpd	
	To analyse MySQL database server log file	Mysqld	
	To analyse login records file.	utmp/wtmp	
	To analyse yum command usage.	Yum	
	To analyse kernel ring buffer information.	Dmesg	

Sl. No.	Use Cases	Event Type	Correlation Rule
	Linux/Unix Common OS Logs		
	Windows System Events		
2	Detect & analyse the failed access requests by users & applications.	Failure Audit	Detect unusual OS incidents
	Detect &analyse the successful access requests by users & applications.	Success Audit	
	Detect &analyse warning messages by the Operating System.	Warning.	
	Detect & analyse the information logs by Operating System.	Information.	
	Detect & analyse critical OS issues.	Error	

Table 29 Operating System - Recommended Use Cases and Correlation Rules

Proxy

Proxy servers intercept the connection from endpoints to the target destination and thus limit direct connection between them. The proxies can be configured as content filtering solutions. Typically, forward proxy servers are configured as content filtering solutions. Reverse proxy servers can act as server load balancing gateways distributing the connection requests to various servers inside the server farm. Sticky connections can be configured for persistent traffic flow to specific servers inside the server farm. The logs generated by both content filtering and reverse proxy servers are relevant from security perspective. So, it is highly important to ensure the smooth integration of proxy servers with SIEM.

Types of Proxy

Gateway: A proxy server that passes requests and responses unmodified.

Forward Proxy: An Internet facing proxy used to forward requests from a wide range of sources.

Reverse Proxy: Internet-facing proxy used as a front-end to control and protect access to a server on a private network.

Event Categories

- Malware / HTTP content inspection
- Web Caching
- Forward & Reverse Proxy Content

Filtering

Recommended Use Cases and Correlation Rules

Sl. No.	Use Case	Event Type	Correlation Rule
1	To analyse the Infected, Suspicious and Encrypted Files reported by malware inspection.	Malware	
	To analyze the Maximum Archive Nesting Exceeded, Maximum Size Exceeded, Maximum Unpacked File Size Exceeded events reported by the Malware Inspection Engine.	Malware/ Size Exceeded	HTTP response blocked
	To analyze the Unknown Encoding, Corrupted File & Time Out events reported by the Malware Inspection Engine.	Malware/ File	HTTP response blocked
	To analyse Malware Inspection Disabled, Malware Inspection Disabled for the Matching Policy Rule, Malware Inspection Disabled for the Matching Web Chaining Rule, Destination Included in Malware Inspection Exceptions List, Response Originated from Proxy Server, Request denied by Malware Inspection Web Filter, Request/Response pair Identified as Exempted Protocol Message & Response Identified as a 200 Response to a CONNECT Request events reported by the Malware Inspection Engine.	Malware/Inspection Status	Malware inspection bypass
2	Identify the frequently accessed web pages by analysing the Proxy Cache Logs.	Cache	Top web pages served

Sl. No.	Use Case	Event Type	Correlation Rule
3	Forward & Reverse Proxy Content Filtering. • Analyse the Proxy logs to identify the users violating the corporate internet download/usage policies. • Monitoring internet usage (overuse or misuse) of employees. • Identify the protocol wise internet usage by the users. • Identify the user attempts to access restricted & malicious websites • Detect DoS attack against the application servers by analysing the no of inbound connections to the server farm through reverse proxy server. • Analyse incoming and outgoing traffic/bandwidth patterns in enterprise network. • Identify top web users, and top websites accessed. • Identify the user attempts to access adult websites. • To analyse the cached objected served by the Proxy server. • Information about requests and responses provided by the Internet web servers • To identify the category wise internet usage. • To analyse access times for various categories of requests. • To identify the policy rules that either allowed or denied access to the request.	PROXY -Content Filtering alerts	Internet usage policy violations Top inbound connections to internal sources by system, user, bandwidth and time. Top outbound connections to external sources by system, user, bandwidth and time. Top outbound DMZ connections to external sources by system, user, bandwidth and time. Bandwidth over consumption. Blocked website access requests

Table 30 Proxy - Recommended Use Cases and Correlation Rules

Storage

All authorized and unauthorized access requests to storage solutions should be monitored by integrating it with a SIEM solution. Below list does not address all the relevant storage use cases a security analyst should develop, however at least this much of uses cases should be there in the SIEM for proper security monitoring.

Recommended Use Cases and Correlation Rules

Sl. No.	Use Case	Event Type	Correlation Rules
1	Detect Zone hopping attacks that targets FC switch weaknesses.	Attack	Fiber Channel Targeted Attacks
2	LUN masking attacks/ WWN spoofing that targets HBA weaknesses.	Attack	LUN targeted Attacks
3	Detect SAN Name server pollution attacks targets FLOGI/PLOGI weaknesses.	Attack	LUN targeted Attacks
4	Detect SAN Man-in-the-Middle attacks that targets Fabric address weaknesses.	Attack	SAN MiTM Attacks

Sl. No.	Use Case	Event Type	Correlation Rules
5	Detect SAN Session hijacking attacks that targets Fibre Channel frame weaknesses.	Attack	SAN session hijacking
6	To analyses the reallocation scans performed recently.	Operation	Suspicious reallocation scans
7	To analyse the storage systems audit logs for Start & Stop of Audit service & attempt for deletion & modification of audit entries. What configuration files were accessed? When the configuration files were accessed? What has been changed in the configuration files? What commands were executed? Who executed the commands? & When the commands were executed?		Storage audit trail corruption

Sl. No.	Use Case	Event Type	Correlation Rules
8	Detect & analyse "forged ICMP redirect" attacks against the storage.	Attack	Storage - "forged ICMP redirect" attacks
9	To analyse the "ping throttling threshold" events reported by the storage solution.	Attack	Storage - "ping throttling threshold"
10	To analyse "Excessive unsupported protocol packets" are being sent to storage system.	Attack	Excessive unsupported protocol packets
11	To analyse the "excessive embryonic TCP connection drops" reported by storage system.	Attack	Excessive embryonic TCP connection drops
12	To identify whether there is any cardholder data or PII stored. To identify whether there is any sensitive authentication data contained in the payment card's storage chip or full magnetic stripe. To identify whether there is any payment card data in payment card terminals or other unprotected endpoint devices, such as PCs, laptops or smart phones.	Data Storage	PCI DSS data storage violation
13	Detect protocol wise access details of the data in storage.	Access	Protocol wise data access

Table 31 Storage - Recommended Use Cases and Correlation Rules

Virtual Private Network

Virtual Private Network gateways provide secure end to end connections between end points. They act as a termination point of secure connection from both static and dynamic end points. Site to Site (S2S) or LAN to LAN VPN connections are always up secure tunnels between gateways. Most of the modern-day firewalls will have VPN capabilities. SSL/TLS, IPSEC etc. are commonly used protocols for VPN. Out of this SSL or TLS based VPN is used for secure dynamic connections from roaming endpoints. IPSEC is a suite of protocols that offers confidentiality and integrity for secure VPN connection. ISAKMP, ESP, AH etc. are the commonly used protocols for IPSEC.ISAKMP is responsible for maintenance and termination of a secure channel over unsecure medium. Data is sent over the secure channel built by ISAKMP with additional protection of ESP or AH.ESP offers both confidentially and integrity services. You may setup VPN with ESP alone or by using a combination of ESP and AH for data protection. To have better visibility of VPN activities you need to integrate VPN gateways with SIEM.SSL multiplexers either integrated within firewall or running in separate gateways split the SSL or HTTPS connection packet inspection. You may integrate SSL multiplexers with your security analytics solutions for improved visibility of events related to data sent over secure SSL/HTTPS channel.

Recommended Use Cases and Correlation Rules

Sl. No.	Use Case	Event Type	Correlation Rules
1	Identify & Analyse the frequent IKE negotiation failures on the Remote access VPN GW. Identify & Analyse the authentication failures on the Remote access VPN GW. Identify & Analyse multiple denials and successful logins on remote access VPN GW. Identify & Analyse targeted SSL vulnerability attacks on VPN GW's. Identify attacks on IPSEC VPN Gateways configured with aggressive mode. Alert when a virus, spyware or other malware is detected by end-point assessment module of VPN Gateway on a host. Alert when end-point assessment module of VPN Gateway successfully removes a piece of malware on an end host.	VPN reconnaissance /Attack	Targeted SSL vulnerability attacks on VPN GW's

Top successful logins to VPN GW

Top failed logins to VPN GW

IKE Negotiation failures |

Sl. No.	Use Case	Event Type	Correlation Rules
2	Alert when a virus, spyware or other malware is detected by end-point assessment module of VPN Gateway on a host. Alert when end-point assessment module of VPN Gateway successfully removes a piece of malware on an end host. Alert when end-point assessment module of VPN Gateway successfully removes a piece of malware on an end host.	Endpoint AV SCAN	Failed endpoint assessments by VPN GW
3	Identify the VPN tunnel creation by the FW / VPN gateway. Identify the VPN tunnel termination by the FW / VPN gateway or user. Generate alerts for file download over VPN session. Generate alerts for object/resource access over VPN session. Identify the bytes of data transferred over VPN session.	Data transfer	Suspicious data transfer over VPN session

Table 32 Virtual Private Network - Recommended Use Cases and Correlation Rules

Vulnerability Scanner

Timely detection of threats by an SIEM can be enhanced with its integration with vulnerability manager. Relevancy of an identified threat can be verified with the vulnerability data. The overall accuracy of threat detection is thus improved with this integration. Vulnerability management solutions or scanners are added as event sources in SIEM, in addition to the relevancy checking the below set of use cases will help the security analyst in real time threat detection when the vulnerability scanning happens.

Recommended Use Cases and Correlation Rules

Sl. No.	Use Cases	Event Type	Correlation Rules
1	To analyse the asset enumeration status provided by the VA tool.	Enumeration and Fingerprinting	NA
2	To analyse the profiling data of network assets by VA tool. Offline configuration auditing of network devices.	Profiling	NA

Sl. No.	Use Cases	Event Type	Correlation Rules
3	To identify the patch auditing status of the enterprise network	Patch Status	Systems without approved patches
4	To analyses Control Systems Auditing data.	Audit Status	
5	To analyse the PII (personally identifiable information) data stored in enterprise networks.	PII	PII (Personal Identity Information) data storage violations
6	To identify threats like Botnet/Malicious Process, Virus, Worm, Trojan and to analyse the vulnerabilities exist in Web Applications.	Threats	Vulnerability to incident ratio and vulnerability trends. Attacks against vulnerable systems classified by criticality.

Sl. No.	Use Cases	Event Type	Correlation Rules
7	To check the compliance status of the environment.	Compliance	Compliance violations.
8	To check the configuration auditing status of the environment.	Configuration	Configuration Audit Report.

Table 33 Vulnerability Scanner - Recommended Use Cases and Correlation Rules

Review Questions

1) …….. runs directly on the mail server and process spam.

   a) Gateway filters
   b) Mail server integrated filters
   c) Cloud – base spam filter
   d) Client – base spam filter

2) ….. can be misconfigured by the attacker to limit the problem with spam black.

   a) Open relay check
   b) RBL
   c) BAYESIAN Filter
   d) Hashing

3) …… uses user input or calculating the statistical probability of an email spam.

   a) BAYESIAN Filter
   b) RBL
   c) Hashing
   d) Open relay check

4) ……. allows execution of specific application based on predefined policies.

a) Application white listing
b) Application ranking
c) Application black listing
d) White coding

5) ...... can be used for prevention of SQL injection attack.

a) Strict input validation
b) Secure coding policy
c) Power shell tools
d) Content filtering solutions

6) Packet filtering works at ...... layer of OSI model.

a) L1
b) L2
c) L3
d) L4

7) Circuit level gateways works at ...... layer of OSI model.

a) L4
b) L5
c) L6
d) L7

8) ...... is needed for the proper working network behavior analytic tools.

a) Access to centralized active log in database
b) Access to data storage
c) Encrypted secure channel
d) Sand box environment

9) ……. server intercepts the connection for endpoints to the target destination and thus limits direct connection between them.

a) Policy
b) Proxy
c) ACL
d) ACS

10) ESP offers ………….. for IPSEC VPN connection.

a) Integrity
b) Confidentiality
c) Availability
d) Confidentiality and integrity

Answers to Review Questions

Module 1

1) Overall risk and security poster of the business information is critical for Chief Security Officer work role in security center.
2) Access to threat intelligence feeds is recommended for Security Analyst work role.
3) A properly defined service level agreement should cover Missing or in proper handling of SLA, Licensing details of SIEM and Escalation and reprioritization procedure.
4) Constituency is a term used in SOC to represent a set of customers to whom SOC provide services.
5) SOC Analyst is responsible for generalization of the data received from different threat intelligence providers.
6) PCI-DSS mandates minimum data retention of 1years.
7) HIPPA mandates data retention of 6 or 7 years.
8) Retention of lateral movement of an advanced persistent threats needs Cross Correlation.
9) Log rate limiting is a common practice

security practitioner follow to reduce the amount of logs getting aggregated in event sources.

10) Tier – One security monitoring team converts alerts to incidents based in the default threshold settings.

Module 2

1) Poller generates an alert when a specific state is detected and one used for service status detection and data integrity checking.
2) Event collector or aggregator is responsible for gathering information from different sensors.
3) Event log in API Can be used by other application to log security event in check point security management server.
4) Log export API Can be used for real time historical retrieval of logs from checkpoint devices.
5) SIEM can collect Microsoft windows events data in an agent less way using MSWMI.
6) MSRPC does not support retrieval of nonstandard windows logs.
7) In collector initiated event forwarding for centralized windows log collection scalability issues are very common.

8) SDEE with an event query or an event subscription uses SSL to query the SDEE server.
9) The throughput of a SOC solution is binded to the EPS.
10) The speed of event reorganization, event escalation and Event resolution is used to calculate to overall response matrix of a SOC.

Module 4

1) SPAN is recommended for exporting of logs if both NSM and monitoring port are in same switch
2) RSPAN is recommended for exporting of logs if both NSM and monitoring ports are in two different switches
3) WHOIS is commonly used for meta data analysis.
4) SQUERT is used to query SGUIL database backend.
5) BRO is an event engine that converts packet streams into series of higher level events.
6) ARGUS is a powerful real time flow monitor that offers comprehensive data

network auditing.
7) SANCP is commonly used for statistical network statistics analysis.
8) ARGUS can read packets directly from network interface and classify it into network transactions.
9) Extracted content data analysis focuses on high level stream contest and can be used for analysis of video, image and other files exchanged between computers.
10) Transaction data Analysis focuses on requests and responses exchanged between end points.

Module 5

1) Mail server integrated filters runs directly on the mail server and process spam
2) Open relay check can be misconfigured by the attacker to limit the problem with spam black listing.
3) BAYESIAN Filter uses user input for calculating the statistical probability of an email spam.
4) Application white listing allows execution of specific application based on predefined policies.

5) Strict input validation can be used for prevention of SQL injection attack.
6) Packet filtering works at L3 layer of OSI model
7) Circuit level gateways works at L6 layer of OSI model.
8) Access to centralized active log in database is needed for the proper working network behavior analytic tools.
9) Proxy server intercepts the connection for endpoints to the target destination and thus limits direct connection between them.
10) ESP offers Confidentiality and Integrity for IPSEC VPN connection

Glossary

Alert Data - 106
API based –MSWMI - 51
Application proxies - 165
APT – 12, 125
Bandwidth Anomaly Detection - 173
Bayesian filter - 122
CIDEE - 54
CIM - 51
Circuit level gateways - 165
CIRT – 24, 95, 96
Collection points - 10
Common hashing protocols - 130
Compliance Monitoring – 9, 14
Connection Rate Detection - 173
Critical logs- 10
CTA - 18
DAM - 135
Data mining - 125
Distributed Management Task Force - 51
ELA – 50, 51
EOI - 44
EPS – 10, 52, 57
Firewall change management Logs - 166
Firewall logs – 39, 150
Forensic analysis – 18, 38, 95, 111
Forward Proxy - 181
Full Content Data Analysis - 100
Full Packet Captures - 19
Gateway – 46, 120, 165, 181, 192, 193

Hashing or checksums - 121
Honeypot activity alerts - 57
ICSA - 54
In-House SOC – 21, 24
Incident Response - 14
Internal Infrastructure - 21
Intrusion Prevention System – 25, 96
Lateral Movements - 12
LEA - 50
Log rate limiting - 10
Malware analysis - 18
Malware scan related alerts - 57
Microsoft Security Event Log - 52
Network address translation - 165
Network User Behavior Analysis - 172
NSM - 96
Open relay checks - 121
Packet Filtering - 164
PCI-DSS – 13, 20, 140, 205
Reverse Proxy - 181
ROA - 43
ROI - 21
Root kit detection - 126
RSPAN - 97
SANCP - 112
Sand boxing - 125
SDEE -54
SDN - 11
Security monitoring - 95
Session Statistics information - 19

Signature based detection - 126
Single Sign-On Solution - 153
SLA – 23, 61
SME – 27, 28
SMS – 50, 51
Snort and Suricata - 106
SOC Manager - 28
SOC Roles – 16, 26, 29
Spam solution alerts - 57
SPAN - 98
Statistical Data Analysis - 105
Syslog packets - 11
Talent acquisition - 29
Threat Intelligence Integration – 15, 38
Threat Mitigation - 14
Transaction data analysis - 103
TIP - 39
Virtual Private network – 165, 192
WBEM - 51
Web proxy logs - 39
Xplico - 111

Index of Tables

Table 1 Regulatory / Compliance Standards and Retention Periods..................13
Table 2 SOC Roles....................27
Table 3 Information Needed by SOC Roles............30
Table 4 Sample OSSEC Syslog Configuration........49
Table 5 Managed SIEM Appliance Incident Notifications.......................65
Table 6 Managed Log Monitoring Incident Notifications.......................66
Table 7 Standard changes related to Managed Device/service..................67
Table 8 Managed Device/service Outage Notifications.......................67
Table 9 Other changes related to Managed Device/service..................68
Table 10 Service Uptime assurance of Managed Device/Service..................69
Table 11 Managed device replacement notification 70
Table 12 Managed Vulnerability Scanning Incident Notifications.......................70
Table 13 Access Control Performance Matrix and Assured Deliverables..................74
Table 14 Boundary Defenses Performance Matrix and Assured Deliverables 78
Table 15 Network and System Resource Integrity Performance Matrix and Assured Deliverables.. 86
Table 16 Host Defenses Performance Matrix and

Assured Deliverables 89
Table 17 Malware Control Performance Matrix and
    Assured Deliverables 91
Table 18 Recommended Use Cases and Correlation
    Rules 125
Table 19 Recommended Use Cases and Correlation
    Rules 130
Table 20 End-point threat protection /
    Application control / Whitelisting solution -
    Recommended Use Cases and Correlation
    Rules 134
Table 21 Web/Application Server or Database -
    Recommended Use Cases and Correlation
    Rules 139
Table 22 Data Loss Prevention / File Integrity
    Monitor - Recommended Use Cases and
    Correlation Rules 144
Table 23 Financial Application 149
Table 24 Host Based Firewall - Recommended Use
    Cases and Correlation Rules 153
Table 25 Single Sign-On Solution - Recommended
    Use Cases and Correlation Rules 157
Table 26 Intrusion Detection/Prevention System
    - Recommended Use Cases and Correlation
    Rules 163
Table 27 Network Based Firewall - Recommended
    Use Cases and Correlation Rules 172
Table 28 Network User Behavior Analysis (NUBA)
    - Recommended Use Cases and Correlation
    Rules 178

Table 29 Operating System - Recommended Use Cases and Correlation Rules............................180
Table 30 Proxy - Recommended Use Cases and Correlation Rules 187
Table 31 Storage - Recommended Use Cases and Correlation Rules 192
Table 32 Virtual Private Network - Recommended Use Cases and Correlation Rules....................198
Table 33 Vulnerability Scanner - Recommended Use Cases and Correlation Rules...........................200

Index of Figures

Figure 1 SIM / SIEM Architecture........................... 19
Figure 2 Xplico Interface...103
Figure 3 Bro Alerts 104
Figure 4 Sguil Session data analysis output............104
Figure 5 Wireshark endpoint statistics....................105

Made in the USA
Monee, IL
23 March 2020